D0248550

DISCOVERING ANGELS

*WISDOM *HEALING *DESTINY*

CHRISTINE ASTELL

IMAGES SUPPLIED BY
BRIDGEMAN ART LIBRARY

DUNCAN BAIRD PUBLISHERS

LONDON

Discovering Angels
Christine Astell

Dedication
**This book is dedicated to all the wonderful beings,
both human and Divine, who have lovingly guided
me along my journey. Thank you.**

First published in the United Kingdom
and Ireland in 2005 by
Duncan Baird Publishers Ltd
Sixth Floor
Castle House
75–76 Wells Street
London W1T 3QH

Conceived, created and designed by
Duncan Baird Publishers

Copyright © Duncan Baird Publishers 2005
Text copyright © Christine Astell 2005
For copyright of photographs see page 160, which are
to be regarded as an extension of this copyright.

The right of Christine Astell to be identified as
the Author of this text has been asserted in accordance
with the Copyright, Designs and Patents Act of 1988.

All rights reserved. No part of this book may be reproduced
in any form or by any electronic or mechanical means,
including information storage and retrieval systems, without
permission in writing from the publisher, except by
a reviewer who may quote brief passages in a review.

Managing Editor: Naomi Waters
Editors: Siobhan O' Connor, Peter Bently
Managing Designer: Dan Sturges
Designer: Clare Thorpe
Picture Editor: Julia Brown

British Library Cataloguing-in-Publication Data:
A CIP record for this book is available from the
British Library.

10 9 8 7 6 5 4 3 2

ISBN-10: 1-84483-097-7   ISBN-13: 9-781844-830978

Typeset in Perpetua
Colour reproduction by Colourscan, Singapore
Printed in Singapore by Imago

Note on abbreviations:
BCE (Before the Common Era) is the equivalent of BC.
CE (Common Era) is the equivalent of AD.

Page 2: *The Coronation of the Virgin* (detail) *c*.1434,
by Fra Angelico (*c*.1387–1455).
Page 5: An angel depicted in an Egyptian tapestry (detail)
from the late fifth century.

DISCOVERING ANGELS

CONTENTS

WHY ANGELS, AND WHY NOW?

Angels are the essence of infinite love and compassion for humankind. Their gifts can be of great benefit to all of us who are prepared to receive them.

To many people angels are powerful and enduring symbols of love, compassion and kindness. To many others, they may seem little more than quaint, almost fairy-tale characters. In today's increasingly secular society, working with angels may not appear the most obvious solution when trying to relieve the stresses of everyday life, or give your life greater meaning. Nevertheless, more and more people are now discovering the true power and meaning of these celestial beings, and seeking to bring them into their lives. This book will describe the lore of several major traditions, as well as showing how angels can act as agents for our spiritual healing and growth.

There are thousands of documented eye-witness accounts, from biblical times to the present day, describing encounters between humans and angels. These days they are often an element of what are referred to as near-death experiences. But in today's rational, material world, the rest of us often refuse to accept things without physical proof. While this has been the driving force behind the discovery of much scientific knowledge, there are some dimensions of existence that we simply have to choose to believe in, or not. This is the very definition of faith, and it is faith that comes into play when you choose to work with angels. After an angelic encounter, it is impossible to

RIGHT: A sixth-century Byzantine mosaic of four angels with the symbols of the Evangelists (the apostles who wrote the Christian Gospels).

dissuade people from believing that they have witnessed angels, so real and powerful has the experience been for them.

Many first-hand accounts share a common theme: the experience leaves the recipient with a profound sense of a Divine Presence. People describe a real and moving feeling of connection with a source of love so intense that it has almost been painful. Encounters with angels are often described as "other-

RIGHT: Stained-glass window, 1870, made by William Morris's factory, removed from St James's Church, Brighouse, West Yorkshire, England, before its demolition.

worldly". What remains is an overwhelming feeling of spiritual love and a renewed sense of well-being. The experience often leaves the seeker with a desire to transcend the mundane aspects of life and turn to what they see as a more meaningful spiritual path.

Angels are inseparable from the Source, Divine Creator, God — whatever you wish to call this divine power. They are also indivisible from their witnesses once their presence has been felt — one cannot separate the observer from the observed. For those of us who need hard evidence, of course, the angels do not leave footprints.

It is probably

true to say that the people most likely to have a mystical or angelic experience are those with an open heart. Not everyone will have the dramatic angelic visions of famous historical accounts, but we can all, if we have this open-hearted attitude, invite the angels into our lives and gradually begin to feel the benefits of their presence and love.

During the past 30 years or so there has been a remarkable resurgence in the popularity of angels. What may seem rather surprising to sceptics is that this trend, far from fizzling out, has only increased in popularity over time. We began a new millennium with angels everywhere. Going well beyond the angels depicted on Christmas cards, we now have angels, or images of them, available to us in almost every capacity – angels to help us in our daily lives, angels to aid with healing, and angels with messages for us. There is now a wide range of angel collectibles and paraphernalia, all sought out by angel lovers.

But the trivialization of these celestial beings is something to be avoided. Angels are spiritual beings of immense intensity, wisdom and devotion. They can bring great joy; they can heal deep wounds; they encourage respect for the planet earth, and love of all creatures. Most of all, they represent the inner peace that can come with a reconnection to the love of God, or the Source. We have a vast capacity to love. The angels can help us tap this potential.

"I am well aware that many will say that no one can possibly speak with spirits and angels as long as he lives in the body; and many will say that it is all imagination, ... and others will make other objections. But by all this I am undeterred, for I have seen, I have heard, I have felt."

Emanuel Swedenborg (1688–1772)

"Angels can fly because they take themselves lightly."

G.K. Chesterton (1874—1936)

The golden angelic thread weaving throughout all the major religions – Buddhism, Christianity, Islam, Judaism – is one of pure, unconditional love. The most amazing sense of relief and light-heartedness arises when we accept that angels are a reality; that they have always existed and continue to do so. But you do not need to subscribe to any particular faith to work with angels. In an age when people have become increasingly disillusioned with some of the organized religions, the love of the angels – which transcends all boundaries of doctrine and dogma – can help us find our own individual spiritual path.

Once we start working with the angels, we find that our lives have more direction and purpose; we notice the kindness of strangers; we discover greater depths within ourselves. Our lives do not always change suddenly and dramatically, but solutions to everyday problems can become clearer; we can connect to a deeper source of love and inner peace, and we can appreciate our place in the universe.

This book is an attempt to bridge the gap between traditional and religious concepts of angels, and contemporary notions derived largely from Theosophical and New Age thinking. It is not necessary to believe all the religious theology that has developed around angels – theology which, after all, was a product of its time, and which evolved in a society far more patriarchal and conservative than our own. But it is helpful to have an understanding of where belief in angels comes from, and where it is leading us to. The second part of the book contains meditations and exercises to provide a practical means of tapping into the energy of specific archangels. We can indeed work with these majestic agents of God – so long as we do so with a pure heart and the right intentions.

LEFT: *Christ in the Sepulchre Guarded by Angels (detail)*, by **William Blake (1757–1827).**

THE ANGEL'S CLARION CALL

Angels are pure love, peace and joy — more real than the most intense emotion, more powerful than any physical force. Opening our hearts to receive the energy of angels can be a transformative experience.

When I first became interested in opening a healing centre for contact with angels, my life was suddenly filled with them. They cropped up in conversations, on TV and radio, in books and magazines, and all around me, in a way that could not be mere chance. Many people might describe this by the fashionable term "synchronicity" – a cluster of meaningful coincidences – but to me this was simply a divine reassurance that my destiny was clear. The more I absorbed myself in my angelic quest, the more it became apparent to me, from these signs as well as from my increased spiritual well-being, that I had taken precisely the right turning in life, at precisely the right time. I was en route to a place filled with healing energies, certificated by the highest authority of all – the Divine.

Thus was I led into the academic world of researching world religions, tracing that thread of angelic presence that runs through our various cultures and belief systems. Yet in all this time of academic endeavour I have always felt it important to stress the fact that the angels offer a direct and universal charge of healing, illumination, protection, joy, peace, wisdom and love. Such powerful energies do not need to be mediated by tradition, with all its esoteric lore: they can be received direct into the heart, like a jolt of divine electricity. I received that wonderful transforming jolt. Anyone can: all it takes is an open heart.

RIGHT: *An Angel Playing a Flageolet* **(detail) by Sir Edward Burne-Jones (1833–1898).**

SYMBOL AND REALITY

The image of the winged angel translates the intensity of angelic experience into a language of the eye and mind — one that however moving and persuasive can only be a faint echo of the truth of the heart.

Certain symbols hold importance to those of us who believe in the reality of the spirit. One example might be the Christmas star over Bethlehem; another, the bodhi tree beneath which the Buddha preached his first sermon.

Such symbols, exerting their powerful fascination, might seem to belong to psychology as much as the realm of faith. They might strike us as cousins to the archetypes identified by the Swiss psychologist Carl Jung — images that create such a powerful response in our unconscious minds that they surface in our dreams.

The sceptic might choose to see angels too as symbols, a visual summary of the healing and purity we yearn for. Yet to treat angels as symbols in this way is to place a barrier between ourselves and the real possibility that

LEFT: A detail from *The Madonna di Ognissanti* **(c.1310), by Giotto (c.1266–1337).**

"An angel can illumine the thought and mind of man by strengthening the power of vision, and by bringing within his reach some truth which the angel himself contemplates."

St Thomas Aquinas (c.1225—74)

14

LEFT: **A detail from an altarpiece of the Virgin of the Aballa Conca, by Pere Serra (fl. 1357–1405).**
OVERLEAF: *Night with her Train of Stars* **(detail) (1919), by Edward Robert Jones (1851–1914).**

is available to us – to feel and benefit from the loving touch of the Divine. Only by being willing to accept that angels have a real, and not merely a symbolic presence, can we access their powers within our lives.

Anyone who has difficulty with this leap of faith may perhaps be hampered, rather than helped, by the traditional portrayal of an angel as a winged creature that is time-honoured within our culture – and not least by such obviously theatrical (though thoroughly commendable) manifestations as the school nativity play. Art, being a visual medium, inevitably deals in symbols and surfaces. Yet look behind – or within – those and you may well discern a glimmer at least of the intensity of a real-life angelic encounter. Read the scriptures and look at angel paintings with humility and wonder – in the knowledge that the reality is infinitely greater.

ANGELS IN
MANY GUISES

Angels can be found in many guises
throughout human history. They appear
across cultures and across religions,
whether it be in the Christian scriptures,
the mystic writings of the Judaic
Kabbalah, the ancient beliefs of
Zoroastrianism, or the tenets of Islam.

LEFT: *The Concert of Angels* (detail) by **Gaudenzio
Ferrari (1474–1546)** in the Sanctuary of Santa
Maria delle Grazie, Saronno, Italy.

ANGELS OF SCRIPTURE

Angels play an important role in
the scriptures of the three great
monotheistic religions — Judaism,
Christianity and Islam — and similar
beings are also found in other
traditions. They appear as a body
of spiritual beings that dwell in the
heavens close to God, who created them
to serve as intermediaries between
the divine and human worlds.

LEFT: *The Ascension of Christ*, **Pietro Perugino
(c.1445–1523). A host of angels and cherubs
escort Christ to heaven in glory.**

WHAT ARE ANGELS?

Angels have been defined as divine messengers, ministering spirits, and attendant or guardian beings. Often described as winged, they have appeared through the ages in many forms, performing a variety of tasks for their Creator.

The word "angel" comes from the Greek *aggelos*, "messenger", which in turn is an interpretation of the biblical Hebrew *malakh*. But while heavenly beings often serve as messengers from God to humankind in the Jewish and Christian scriptures, this is not their only function. In the Judaeo-Christian tradition the term "angel" is given to a wide range of powerful beings that act as God's agents and attendants. In the centuries before Christ, Jewish writers came to see God as wholly transcendent, invisible and unknowable, dwelling in the furthest heavens. Exceptional people like the prophet Enoch, who was

"And I saw countless angels — a hundred thousand times a hundred thousand, ten million times ten million — encircling the house of God. Michael, Raphael, Gabriel, Phanuel and numerous other holy angels that are in heaven above, go in and out of that house."

The First Book of Enoch, 71.8

transported to the heavens, could have direct contact with the divine, but otherwise God communicated with humanity through intermediaries – primarily the angels. The universe was understood to be full of a vast number of angelic beings that even controlled natural phenomena like the stars and the weather, all operating under God's authority. Later, hierarchies were devised to impose order on the many types of angels, with the seraphim and cherubim at the top and "ordinary" messenger angels at the bottom.

Celestial beings that fulfil many of the roles of angels are found in other traditions, from ancient Egypt to Islam. Like angels, they served as links between the divine and humankind.

BELOW: **A detail from** *The Annunciation*, **Leonardo da Vinci (1452–1519), showing the Archangel Gabriel in Renaissance-style dress.**

DO ANGELS HAVE BODIES?

Our ideas about what angels look like come from a variety of visionary accounts. These describe angelic visitors in many ways, from beings in human-like form to ethereal presences without physical substance.

When angels appear in the Bible they sometimes manifest in human form, as when Abraham welcomes three angelic guests who at first seem to be ordinary travellers (Genesis 18). Later, two of the angels go to stay in Sodom, where again they are taken for human visitors (Genesis 19), and Jacob wrestles with a very physical angel in Genesis 32.

At times angels can take a basically human form but with unusual features, such as the being in Daniel 10.6 with arms and legs like polished metal and precious stones, and a gleaming face with glowing eyes. The prophet Ezekiel describes four celestial creatures — he later calls them cherubim — that are part human and part beast: "They were of human form. Each had four faces, and each of them had four wings. Their legs were straight, and the soles of their feet were like the sole of a calf's foot; and they sparkled like burnished bronze. Under their wings on their four sides they had human hands" (Ezekiel 1.5–8). The prophet goes on to say that the faces of each being were

those of a man, an ox, an eagle and a lion. The same four beings reappear, in a slightly different form, in the Book of Revelation (4.6–8).

But usually the Bible is less explicit about what angels look like, and there has long been a debate as to whether angels have a physical form at all. Angels were sometimes said to resemble humans but were more often envisioned as hybrid beings, or as abstract and formless – for example, as emanations of pure light.

In his letter to the Hebrews, Paul said that God "makes his angels winds, his servants flames of fire" (Hebrews 1.7). Eventually, both Jews and Christians concluded that "angels take different forms at the bidding of their master, God", as St John of Damascus (675–749CE) put it.

The idea of angels having wings no doubt comes from the descriptions of Ezekiel and other scriptural passages. The first depictions of angels had stubby wings or none at all, and it was a relatively long time – not until the fourth century CE – before wings became a more or less fixed feature of angels in Christian art. Judaism forbids "any likeness of anything that is in heaven above" (Exodus 20). The beautiful angels in

ABOVE and LEFT: The frescoes by Giotto (*c.*1266–1337) in the Scrovegni Chapel in Padua, Italy, show numerous winged angels lamenting overhead during Christ's Passion.

famous scenes such as the Annunciation are almost always shown with wings, although wings are not mentioned in the Gospels.

Early artists used images of the Greek and Roman gods – especially Eros, or Cupid as the Romans knew him, the winged god of love – as the inspiration for their representations of angels. It was a few more centuries, however, before angels acquired the magnificent swan-like wings familiar to us from medieval and Renaissance art.

ANGELS OF ANTIQUITY

The Western concept of angels has its roots in the Judaeo-Christian tradition. But heavenly messengers and intermediaries are also found in the older civilizations that surrounded the ancient biblical lands.

The first angels mentioned in the Bible are the cherubim, which God sets at the east of Eden to prevent Adam and Eve from returning to paradise after their expulsion (Genesis 3.24). The word cherubim may derive from the Assyrian *karibu*, the name given to a fierce winged protective spirit or deity. With the body of a bull or other beast and a human head, the *karibu* guarded the entrances not only to temples but also to people's homes. "Angels" in the form of four-winged human figures also feature in Assyrian religion as protective spirits, as depicted, for example, in reliefs from the palace of King Sargon II (721–705BCE).

But angel-like beings are older even than this, and can be traced back nearly five thousand years to Sumer, probably the world's first civilization. Sumerian beliefs may lie behind the "sons of God" who descend to Earth to couple with women in Genesis 6. These were interpreted by later writers as angels, and their monstrous offspring, the giant Nephilim, as the fallen angels or demons that were the source of the world's evils. In Sumerian belief, the heavenly messengers are called *igigi* (spirits of heaven) and are also sometimes described as the "sons" or "ministers" of the gods. The benevolent *igigi* have their counterpart in the malevolent *anuna-ki* who dwell, like the fallen angels, under the earth.

The Babylonians, who ruled Mesopotamia after the Sumerians from about 1850 to 900BCE,

RIGHT: **A detail from an Assyrian stone frieze, dating from the eighth century BCE, showing a four-winged protective spirit.**

had their own equivalent of the *igigi* in the *sukalli*, sent from the heavens to declare the will of the gods and carry out divine commands.

In Canaanite myths, written down about three and a half millennia ago, powerful deities such as the gods El and Baal communicated through divine messengers. The Canaanites wrote their name as *mlkm*, which is the equivalent of the Hebrew *malakhim* – the word that was rendered in Greek as *aggelos* (messenger). The *mlkm* also ran errands between the gods and humans, much like their angelic counterparts. The name of El, the Canaanite supreme god, is the same as the suffix *-el* (of God), that appears in the names of Gabriel and the other archangels.

Divine winged beings are also found in ancient Egypt – in fact, in Egyptian symbolism wings are virtually synonymous with heavenly protection. The god Horus was often simply represented as a sun-disk with wings, a protective symbol that adorned temple ceilings, gateways and private memorials throughout Egypt. The mother of Horus, the goddess Isis, was often shown as having protective wings. She appears in tombs and coffins with wings outspread over the body of the deceased, and is shown, with her winged sister Nephthys, behind the throne of the king.

It may or may not be significant that Isis means "throne" – the name given to one of the three highest orders of angels (see pages 78–85). The Egyptians also believed that the dead could visit the land of the living as a *ba*, or "soul", a creature with the face of the deceased and the body of a bird. With the right prayers and rituals, the winged *ba* could become an *akh* (effective spirit), a sort of guardian angel with semi-divine powers to intercede in the human world and protect the living from harm.

Christian depictions of angels owe more to the dominant classical culture of the early Christian centuries. The first artists to represent angels used common images of Greek and Roman gods as their models, and the

Greeks and Romans had often attributed wings to divine and semi-divine beings.

In Greek myth Hermes, the son of the supreme god Zeus, was the messenger of the gods and bore their words to humankind. He moved swiftly on winged sandals, wearing a messenger's hat that is often also shown with wings, and bearing the staff of a herald. He and Aphrodite were the parents of Eros, the god of love, who was represented as a beautiful winged youth. In Roman myth Eros was called Amor

ABOVE: **This Greek vase (detail, left) from the eighth century BCE, shows Hermes holding his messenger's staff, called a** *caduceus*.

(Love) or Cupid, whom Roman artists depicted as a winged infant – an image that evolved into the angelic cupids or *putti* of Christian art.

The Romans also believed that everyone had a benign personal guardian spirit, called a *genius* for a man and a *juno* for a woman, who accompanied them from the cradle to the grave.

THE HINDU DEVAS

Celestial beings that fulfil many functions of angels are not confined to the ancient Near East. They may also be found in the religions that originated in India in the millennium before Christ.

Hinduism possesses a host of heavenly beings that closely resemble angels in a number of ways. As well as the *mahadevas* and *mahadevis* – the great gods and goddesses like Shiva, Vishnu and Durga – there are countless other lesser divinities, or *devas*. The *devas* first appear in the Vedas, the most ancient Indian scriptures, where they are linked with the natural world and the elements, such as the weather and fire. They exist alongside the *asuras*, similar beings who are connected with moral concepts such as friendship and marriage. However, the *devas* and *asuras* came to be seen increasingly as rivals, and in later Hinduism they have become

enemies: the *devas* protecting the world from the malice and mischief of the *asuras* – much as the angelic host are said to be vigilant and active against the fallen angels or demons.

Deva means "radiant being", and as the name suggests *devas* are conceived as having not a physical form but bodies of light or "refined energy". Like angels, though, they may appear in human form when they descend from the Devaloka, the divine realm, to the material realm of humankind. In Indian art, they are often depicted with very human characteristics.

Like angels, *devas* intervene in the human world to bring divine blessings and assistance to those in need. As one modern Hindu writer (anonymous) has put it, "*devas* are able to perform many wondrous feats, are imbued with love, and live only to serve God and other souls." There are various types of Hindu *devas*, including *devas* who preside over sacrifice, *devas* who destroy pain, and 33 *devas* who are especially powerful helpers of humankind and have their own special realm, the Heaven of the Thirty Three, within the Devaloka.

Buddhism began in India and incorporated the ancient belief in *devas* into its ideas of *karma* and rebirth. Those who lived impeccable lives on earth could aspire to be reborn as a *deva*. They are still trapped in the cycle of rebirth, but are higher up in the celestial pantheon by virtue of their good deeds in previous lives. The Buddha himself was reborn as a *deva* in his penultimate life before his final rebirth as Siddhartha. Thus the *devas* are regarded as fully real

and possess superhuman powers, though they are subservient to the Buddha.

Buddhist *devas*, however, generally do not tend to intervene in human affairs, unlike *bodhisattvas*, enlightened beings devoted to becoming Buddhas. They are dedicated to helping all living creatures and have sometimes been called "Buddhist angels".

RIGHT AND LEFT: Indian *devas* take on a variety of colourful forms, as shown in these 19th-century depictions. Agni (left) is a deity of fire and serves as the messenger of the gods.

PERSIAN ANGELS

The angel-like beings in Zoroastrianism form a fascinating link between the devas of Hinduism and the angels of the Judaeo-Christian tradition.

In the ancient Zoroastrian religion of Persia appear seven powerful angelic beings known as the *amesha spentas* (bounteous immortals), who have been compared to the archangels – the "seven who stand before God" – in the Book of Revelation. Each of the *amesha spentas* represents an aspect of the Zoroastrian God, Ahura Mazda (Wise Lord), and is understood to be both a powerful agent of God and a moral and religious principle to be followed by devotees. They are named as Khshathra Vairya (Desirable Rule, Kingdom of God); Haurvatat (Wholeness of Health); Spenta Armaiti (Rightmindedness, Devotion); Ameretat (Immortality); Vohu Manah (Good Thinking, Good Mind); Spenta Mainyu (Bounteous Spirit, Wise Lord); and Asha Vahishta (Right, Truth and Order). In his writings – which he claimed were delivered to him by an angel nine times human size – the prophet Zoroaster (Zarathustra) (*c*.628–551 BCE), frequently addresses the *amesha spentas* directly in prayer and calls for their assistance.

Ranking below the *amesha spentas* are the *yazatas* (adorable ones), angelic beings that may take both male and female forms. There are said to be at least 40 of them and they are divided into two types. Those responsible for the spiritual and moral dimension (wisdom, charity, and so on), are called Celestial Adorable Ones, and those who oversee material and natural phenomena, such as air, earth, wind and fire, are called the Material Adorable Ones.

A third rank of Zoroastrian angel is formed by the *fravashi* (guardian spirits). Every person is said to be accompanied from birth to death by a *fravashi*, who acts as a personal helper, protector, healer, guide and conscience. According to Zoroaster, a *fravashi* is "strong and vigilant, an armed and armoured warrior."

Each of the *amesha spentas* had its rival malevolent being. In Zoroastrian teachings there are many demons, led by Angra Mainyu, or Ahriman, the Lord of Darkness. Persian influence on Judaic (and later, Christian) concepts of angels originates in the time of the Persian domination of the Near East from the 6th to 4th centuries BCE.

There is also a connection between the *devas* and *asuras*, the "angels" and demons of ancient India, and Zoroastrian beliefs. The roles, though, are reversed: in Zoroastrianism the *ahuras* are the blessed beings or angels, and the *devas* their demonic adversaries.

LEFT: **Similar to depictions of Christ's Ascension, this 16th-century Persian painting shows the Ascension of Muhammad, surrounded by angels.**

JUDAEO-CHRISTIAN ANGELS

Angels are mentioned directly or indirectly nearly three hundred times in the Old and New Testaments. They are portrayed as a vast body of celestial beings, somewhere between God and humans.

Like humankind, angels were created (Psalm 148.5, Colossians 1.16), although the book of Genesis says nothing about their creation. This and other "gaps" in the Bible were filled by the writers of the Pseudepigrapha – works written between around 350BCE and 300CE that were not accepted as scripture by either Jews or Christians. Thus the Book of Jubilees (second century BCE) declares that angels were created on the first day, immediately following the creation of the heavens, earth and waters. This view was later officially accepted by the Christian Church in the Middle Ages.

Angels appear in the Bible most often as God's messengers, communicating his will to humankind. In Genesis alone, an angel finds Hagar in the wilderness; angels announce to Abraham that his elderly wife will bear a son, and angels tell Lot to flee Sodom before God destroys it (Genesis 16–19). Elsewhere in the Old Testament, an angel tells Gideon that he will save his people, foretells the birth of Samson, and appears to the prophet Daniel. In the New Testament, the angel Gabriel announces the births of both John the Baptist and Christ, and tells the shepherds to go to Bethlehem. There are many other instances of angelic utterances, some of which occur in dreams or as an "inner voice" inspiring the revelations of a prophet.

As St Augustine pointed out in the fifth century, the word "angel" itself (the Greek *aggelos*, meaning "messenger") describes just one of the angels' functions and not their fundamental nature. In Judaeo-Christian belief they exist primarily as attendants on the throne of God, perpetually serving and praising him. The vision of the prophet Daniel vividly describes the heavenly court, in which "a thousand thousands served him, and ten thousand times ten thousand stood attending him" (Daniel 7.9–10). The book of Job declares that "the heavenly beings shouted for joy" when God laid the foundations of the earth (Job 38.4–7). There are numerous references to "the seven angels who stand before God", as the Book of Revelation (8.2) puts it, who appear to be an inner circle of angels that surround the divine throne. They have often been identified with the seven archangels, or "great angels". In the Bible only two of the archangels,

Gabriel and Michael, are named (and the word archangel itself is only found in the New Testament, where it occurs twice). The name of another archangel, Raphael, is found in the apocryphal book of Tobit. The names of the other four archangels are found in various versions of the non-canonical Jewish writings, such as the First Book of Enoch. In the vision of Enoch, the seven "holy angels who watch" are named as Suruel (or Uriel), Raphael, Raguel, Michael, Saraqael, Gabriel and Remiel.

The archangels are one of several categories of angel that Judaeo-Christian tradition identifies in the scriptures. The early Church identified seven more categories (see pages 74–89), including

LEFT: **The angels of the Ark of the Covenant, as shown in a 13th-century illumination of Hebrew texts.**

35

the cherubim (named in Genesis 3 and Ezekiel 10) and seraphim (named in Isaiah 6). The non-canonical writings classify the angels into a large number of different groups according to their areas of responsibility. So, in addition to angels who control natural phenomena there are figures such as "the angel of peace" and "the angel of death", as well as a whole range of celestial beings whose main function is to guard God's heavenly throne. These are not really distinguishable from the angels except that they have distinctive names, such as the seraphim, cherubim and ophannim.

Such names and classifications vary considerably from one author to another. A notable feature of these writings not found in the Bible is the idea of angels structured within a hierarchy, often headed by the archangels. Many Christians later accepted the idea of an angelic hierarchy that ranked the various types of angel identified in the Bible, in particular the

LEFT: **An angel from *The Adoration of the Shepherds* (detail), by Jorg Stocker (1481–1525), showing exquisitely coloured wings.**

hierarchy devised in the 5th century by Pseudo-Dionysius (see pages 80–9).

As well as being messengers *from* God, angels in the non-biblical tradition also actively interceded for individuals and conveyed prayers *to* heaven. Another important angelic role was to guard the righteous against the wicked. Angels frequently tested humans to prove their loyalty to God, and incapacitated evil spirits that might lead them astray.

The Essenes, a Jewish sect that was active around the time of Christ (see pages 97–9), apparently had to take a vow to preserve the names of angels. Angels came to play a key role in other mystical and esoteric traditions, such as the Judaic Merkabah and Kabbalah. Merkabah mysticism even speaks of humans becoming angels – Enoch is said to have so pleased God that he was transformed into Metatron, a mighty archangel (see pages 154–7).

ANGELS OF THE APOCALYPSE

Angels appear throughout the scriptures. But they play a particularly important role in the writings known as apocalyptic scripture, in which special chosen individuals receive visions of the heavens.

The term apocalypse (revelation) is given to Jewish and Christian writings in which God reveals cosmic events and phenomena — usually what will happen at the end of time — through angels, visions or dreams. The genre takes its name from the most famous work of this type, the Apocalypse, or Book of Revelation in the New Testament. St John the Divine declares how he "fell down to worship at the feet of the angel" who had given him his

* * * * * * * * * * * * * * * * * *

"Then I saw an Angel coming down from heaven, holding in his hand the key to the bottomless pit and a great chain."

Revelation 20:1

visions (Revelation 22.8). Much of Revelation describes a vision of the Last Day of Judgment, in which seven angels will blow their trumpets, each blast heralding a different disaster to be visited on the humans who have not been marked with God's seal on their foreheads.

The First Book of Enoch was the most influential apocalypse outside the Bible. It recounts Enoch's tour of the cosmos, with the archangel Uriel as his guide, and is one of the earliest works to put the number of archangels at seven. Another apocalypse is the Book of Daniel, which, with the vision of Ezekiel, influenced the descriptions of angels in Revelation.

RIGHT: **Archangel Michael weighing souls on the Last Day of Judgment in a detail from an altarpiece by Rogier van der Weyden (1399–1464).**

ANGELS OF ISLAM

Angels have a strong presence in Islamic scripture and law — it was, after all, an angel who dictated the Qur'an, the very word of God, to the Prophet Muhammad.

Belief in angels (*malaikah*) is an article of faith in Islam, and the word *malaikah* occurs more than 80 times in the Qur'an. The Islamic angelic hierarchy resembles the Judaeo-Christian. At the top are the *hamalat al-'Arsh*, the four throne-bearers of Allah, symbolized in Muslim legend by a man, a bull, an eagle and a lion (just as described by Ezekiel, see pp.24–5). Next come the *karibuyin* (cherubim), who perpetually praise Allah. These first angelic beings generally remain in the presence of Allah and do not intervene in the earthly realm, unlike the archangels: Jibril (Gabriel), the giver of revelations; Mikhail (Michael), the provider; Israil or Asrail, the angel of death; and Israfil (Raphael), the angel who will blow the trumpet at the Last Judgment. Two other important angels are Munkar and Nakir, who test the faith of the recently deceased. In addition to these there is a host of lesser angels.

Every individual is said to possess two guardian angels: one to record good deeds, the other to record bad.

Angels have a highly significant role in Islam. For example, Muhammad (571–632CE) taught that there was an angel in charge of every blade of grass, indicating that every aspect of nature, not just humankind, is cared for by the angels: "Every raindrop that falls is accompanied by an angel, for even a raindrop is a manifestation of being" (Qur'an).

The most important individual angel is Jibril. Muhammad was initially unable to identify the being through which he received the divine revelations, and the Qur'an itself names Jibril only three times. Along with Mikhail, Jibril plays a key role in the famous account of the Prophet's night journey to the holy city of Jerusalem, and his ascent from there to the heavens. After first being purified by the two angels, Muhammad was guided by Jibril through the various levels of the heavens until they reached the throne of Allah. Usually, Muhammad did not see Jibril but only heard his voice, although it was said that Jibril once appeared in the form of one of Muhammad's disciples. Elsewhere, Jibril is described as having 600 wings, or as sitting on a chair suspended between heaven and earth. Mikhail has wings of emerald green and resides in

The Head of the Angels of the Sixth Sky (left) and the Head of the Angels of the Seventh Sky (above), from *The Wonders of the Creation and the Curiosities of Existence*, Zakariya'ibn Muhammad al-Qazwini, Islamic School (14th century).

the seventh heaven.

In legend, Jibril and Mikhail were the first to obey when Allah commanded the angels to bow in worship before Adam, a tradition also found in non-biblical Jewish and Christian writings. Islam also records that one of the angels, Shaitan (Satan), refused to pay homage to Adam and as a result was cast out of heaven with his followers.

The Islamic world is occupied not only by humankind, but also by the *jinn* who exist in a kind of parallel universe. The *jinn* were spirits created by Allah before humankind (just like Judaeo-Christian angels), and Muhammad said that while angels were created from light, the *jinn* were made from smokeless fire. Thus their nature has generally been fiery, and this is reflected in their relationship with humanity, whom the *jinn* test, or even possess.

MANIFESTATIONS OF GOD

There are several places in the Bible where "the angel of the Lord" appears to signify the very manifestation of God himself, rather than the appearance of a mere intermediary or messenger.

The best known appearance of "the angel of the Lord" is the story of Moses and the burning bush (Exodus 3). On Mount Horeb, in the wilderness of Midian, "the angel of the Lord" appears to Moses in the burning bush, and subsequently declares "I am the God of your father." Earlier, in Genesis 18, God appears to Abraham in the form of three angels, but as the story goes on the phrase "they said" changes to "the Lord said" (Genesis 18.9–13). Similarly, when an angel visits Gideon in Judges 6, the visitor is alternately spoken of as "the angel of the Lord" and as "the Lord". In Genesis 22

RIGHT: The angel of the Lord speaks to Moses from a burning bush, as shown in this ethereal composition *Moses and the Burning Bush*, by visionary and artist, William Blake (1757–1827).

"the angel of the Lord" intervenes to prevent Abraham from sacrificing his only son, Isaac, to God. And when the angel of the Lord appears in Judges 13 to foretell the birth of Samson, Manoah and his wife anxiously exclaim: "We shall surely die, for we have seen God." Such passages are called theophanies, from the Greek *theo* (God) and *phaneia* (to show oneself), and seem to describe an appearance of God himself, rather than his angelic messenger.

The Greek version of the Old Testament calls the Messiah "the angel of Great Counsel" (Isaiah 9.6); and some Christian thinkers like Tertullian (third century) and the Protestant reformer John Calvin (1509–64) interpreted "the angel of the Lord" to mean the pre-incarnate Christ – the Logos, or "Word", as in John 1.1. The Logos was an expression of God's innermost being, the divine reason projected into speech, the agent of both creation and revelation. The "angel of the Lord" that appeared to Moses and others anticipated the time when God would manifest himself to humankind in fully human form.

✳✳

"There the angel of the Lord appeared to him in a flame of fire out of a bush; he looked, and the bush was blazing, yet it was not consumed. Then Moses said, 'I must turn aside and look at this great sight, why the bush is not burned up.' ... God called to him out of the bush, 'Moses, Moses!' And Moses said 'Here I am.' Then he said, 'Come no closer! Remove the sandals from your feet, for the place on which you are standing is holy ground.' He said 'I am the God of your father, the God of Abraham, the God of Isaac, and the God of Jacob.'"

Exodus 3.2—6

43

ANGELS AS MESSENGERS

The angels of the Bible appear for the most part in the role of God's messengers to humankind. It is through angels that God communicates his will, and foretells and forewarns of momentous events.

In Genesis 16, an angel finds Hagar in the wilderness and announces to her that she will bear a son, Ishmael, who is traditionally said to be the progenitor of the Arabs and other wandering desert tribes. It is probably in the form of an angel that God announces to Abraham his great mission as the patriarch of nations, and tells him that his wife Sarah, who is past the age of childbearing, will nevertheless bear a son (Genesis 18). This is the first of several angelic annunciations of a special birth, in the Hebrew Bible and New Testament, the most famous, of course, being Gabriel's annunciation to the Virgin Mary.

"Angels light the way."

Anonymous, 20th century

Jacob's famous vision in Genesis 28 presents a vivid picture of angels descending to earth and returning to heaven on a celestial ladder. In this case, the angels are the herald of an annunciation by God, who promises Jacob the land for himself and his descendants. Later, in Genesis 32, Jacob wrestles until dawn with a very physical angel, who finally declares that Jacob's name shall henceforth be Israel (God strives, or He who strives with God).

Angels appear in a similar role in the Book of Judges, as when an angel tells Gideon that he will "deliver Israel from the hand of Midian" and save his people (Judges 6). Later, an angelic messenger informs Manoah and his childless wife that she shall "conceive and bear a son" – Samson – who will deliver Israel from the hands of the Philistines (Judges 13).

In the Book of Daniel the angel Gabriel appears to Daniel to explain to him the significance of his apocalyptic vision (Daniel 8 and 9). This is the first time Gabriel is named in the Bible, and he is referred to not as an angel but as "the man Gabriel". In the New Testament, Gabriel features prominently as the angel who announces the births of John the Baptist and Jesus Christ. In Luke's Gospel, Gabriel tells the

BELOW: *The Anunciation* (detail), by Fra Angelico (c.1387–1455), juxtaposes Mary's visitation from Gabriel with Adam and Eve's banishment from the Garden of Eden.

ageing Zechariah that his barren wife Elizabeth will bear a son, John (Luke 1). John is known as the Forerunner of Christ, and this angelic visitation is itself a forerunner to the even more momentous annunciation to Mary later in the first chapter of Luke. Once again, using language recalling similar annunciations in the Old Testament, Gabriel tells Mary that although she is a virgin she will conceive by the Holy Spirit and bear a son. Luke's account is a moving passage of considerable beauty, and not surprisingly the scene of the angel Gabriel before Mary has always been popular with artists. In Matthew's Gospel, the annunciation happens to Joseph rather than Mary. He is betrothed to Mary but she has somehow become pregnant and Joseph sadly resolves to send her away. However, an angel appears to him in a dream to assure him that she has conceived by the Holy Spirit.

Angels make important appearances at other crucial moments in the life of Jesus. After his birth, an angel appears to the shepherds to tell them the "good news of a great joy" (Luke 2.10) and urge them to go to Bethlehem. The

"Are not all angels spirits in the divine service, sent to serve for the sake of those who are to inherit salvation?"

Hebrews 1. 14

unnamed angel is accompanied by "a multitude of the heavenly host praising God" (Luke 2.13). Angels minister to Jesus in the wilderness, and an angel strengthens Christ during his agony in the Garden of Gethsemane. Later still, after the crucifixion, an angel appears to the women at the empty tomb and announces Christ's

resurrection – Matthew says that the angel's "appearance was like lightning, and his clothing white as snow" (Matthew 28.3). In Luke and John, the women see not one but two angelic beings wearing "dazzling clothes" (Luke 24.4).

There are many other instances of divine utterances being delivered by angels in the Bible. Some of these occur in dreams, like the annunciation to Joseph, or as an "inner voice" inspiring the revelations of a prophet. In the original Hebrew, the prophet Zechariah several times mentions "the angel who talked *within* me" when speaking of the revelations he received (Zechariah 1.9 and elsewhere).

Angelic missions are frequently barely more than momentary, but sometimes the angels are sent to a people for a more prolonged period. An example is in Exodus 14, when the "angel of God" in the form of a pillar of cloud travels before the Israelites as they leave Egypt.

LEFT: *The Morning of the Resurrection*, by Edward Burne-Jones (1833–99), shows Mary Magdalene seeing the risen Christ after the two angels told her not to seek the living among the dead.

ENCOUNTERS WITH ANGELS

Throughout history individuals have reported receiving divine guidance from angelic beings. Angels have manifested themselves in a variety of apparently physical forms. At other times they have communicated through meditation, dreams and trances, or as a mysterious, unplaceable and disembodied voice.

LEFT: **Angels in a heavenly landscape, from a cycle of frescoes by Benozzo di Lese di Sandro (1420–97), in the Palazzo Medici-Ricardi, Florence, Italy.**

ANGELS AND PROPHETS

*Many remarkable angelic encounters in the scriptures involved prophets
through whom divine truths were revealed to humankind. Angels
sometimes appeared to them in person, or in inner visions and dreams.*

SPIRITVS·QVOQVE·LEVAVIT·ME
ET·ASSVMSIT·ME·ET·ABII·AMARVS·
IN·INDIGNATIŌE·SPIRITVS·MEI·MA
NVS·ENIM·DNI·ERAT·MECM·ON·TOR
TANS·ME·DIXIT·APERI·OS·TVVM
ET·COMEDE·QVÆ·CVMQVE·DO·TI
BI · EZECHIEL· P·

Throughout the Bible the prophets possess a special knowledge of angels and enjoy a closer relationship with them than other humans. The messengers of the one true God even appear to the prophets of other nations, like the seer Balaam in Numbers 22. In 1 Kings 19, the prophet Elijah flees into the wilderness, where an angel provides him with sustenance for 40 days and nights. At the end of his mission, Elijah is carried to heaven in a whirlwind on an angelic chariot of fire (2 Kings 2.11–12). His successor, Elisha, is surrounded

LEFT: *Ezekiel and the Angel*, **fresco (detail) c.1477, from the Sanctuary of Santa Casa, Loretto, Italy. This "holy house" is believed to be the house in Nazareth in which Jesus grew up, transported to its present location by angels in the 13th century.**

by the Syrians at Dothan, but the "horses and chariots of fire" of the angelic host return to protect him. Only Elisha can see the heavenly host, until he prays to God to let his servant see it too (2 Kings 6.17).

Angels are prominent in the Bible's great prophetic books, especially those in which the prophets receive visions of the heavens and the angelic beings that dwell there. But even prophets like Jeremiah, who do not record specific visions, constantly refer to God as "the Lord of Hosts", the commander of the great angelic army against Israel's oppressors.

Isaiah describes the six-winged seraphim – the first time the word occurs in the Bible – standing above the throne of God and chanting: "Holy Holy Holy is the Lord of hosts; the whole earth is full of his glory" (Isaiah 6.3). The preceding verse in Isaiah 6 is one source for the idea that angels have wings, while the angelic chant above became part of the Christian liturgy. One seraph touches Isaiah's mouth with a purifying burning coal.

The angels in the Book of Ezekiel are even more remarkable. Ezekiel receives the gift of prophecy from God in a vision that begins with the appearance of the "four living creatures", which he describes in detail (see pages 24–5) and later calls cherubim. They appear like gleaming bronze in "a great cloud with brightness around it and fire flashing forth continually" (Ezekiel 1.4). Ezekiel goes on to describe four great whirling wheels, gleaming like chrysolite and with rims "full of eyes", which accompany the cherubim wherever they go (Ezekiel 1.18). Ezekiel says that "the spirit of the living creatures was in the wheels," and later writers identified them as a type of angelic being called a "throne", third in the angelic hierarchy after the seraphim and cherubim (see pages 82–3). Based on Ezekiel's vision, thrones were sometimes said to be the wheels of God's heavenly chariot.

Later, an angel appears to Ezekiel to show him visions of the desecration of the temple of

"His body was like beryl, and his face like lightning, and his eyes like flaming torches ... and the sound of his words like the roar of a multitude."

Daniel, 10.6

Jerusalem and the punishment of the wicked. This angel "had the appearance of a man" but "below what appeared to be his loins it was fire, and above his loins it was brightness, like gleaming bronze". In the course of this angelic vision, the prophet once more sees the four cherubim and the celestial wheels.

The prophet Daniel also has a special relationship with angels. When Daniel's friends, three prominent Jews, are cast into a furnace, an angel protects them from the flames (Daniel 3.25–8). Daniel himself is saved by an angel when jealous plotters cause him to be thrown into the lion's den (Daniel 6.22). In Daniel 4,

he explains the prophecy spoken by an angel in a dream to King Nebuchadnezzar, and in the following chapter he interprets the doom-laden words written on the wall of Belshazzar's banqueting hall by "the fingers of a man's hand" – probably an angel's, because the hand was sent from God's presence (Daniel 5.24).

Much of the Book of Daniel is devoted to Daniel's apocalyptic prophecies. The first is a vision of four great beasts who herald a vision of God himself, the "Ancient of Days", on his throne of flames with "its wheels [of] burning fire" (Daniel 7.9) – recalling the thrones, or angels in the form of wheels, in Ezekiel. The beasts are destroyed and the prophet approaches "one of those who stood there" to find out the meaning of what he has just seen. The angel interprets the beasts as rulers who will oppress Israel, but reassures Daniel that God, "the Most High", will prevail.

An angel also interprets Daniel's next vision, which is similar though not a dream. For

RIGHT: *The Vision of Daniel* (detail), by Scottish artist William Hamilton (1751–1801).

the first time in the Bible, God's messenger is named: it is Gabriel, who has "the appearance of a man" (Daniel 8.15) and in fact is called "the man Gabriel" when he appears a second time (Daniel 9.21). On this occasion he gives Daniel a prophecy of the destruction of Jerusalem by a "desolator", who will himself be destroyed.

Daniel's last vision is delivered by an angel described in Daniel 10 as having a face like lightning, eyes like fire, and limbs like gleaming bronze. He gives Daniel a vision of the "time of the end", culminating in the arrival of the angelic host under Michael – he too is first named in Daniel (10.13). At the end of the vision, the angel is joined by two others in a final affirmation.

There are other angelic appearances to prophets and visionaries in the Bible, notably to Zechariah and the author of the Book of Revelation. Outside the Bible, angels feature very prominently in many Jewish and Christian works that claim a famous prophet as their author but were actually written long after the prophet's time. The best known is the First Book of Enoch (1 Enoch), the oldest parts of which date to around 200BCE. There are fragments of 1 Enoch among the Dead Sea Scrolls, and the work was popular among the early Christians – it is even quoted in the New Testament (Jude 14). But it later fell out of favour with the Church, except in Ethiopia, where it is accepted as scripture. Rediscovered in the West only in the late 18th century, Enoch is today one of our richest sources of ancient Jewish and Christian belief in angels.

Enoch is briefly mentioned in the Old Testament as Adam's sixth descendant. Genesis 5.24 says only that "Enoch walked with God; then he was no more, because God took him." This enigmatic sentence inspired 1 Enoch, and other writings that claim to be the very revelations that God granted to Enoch through the angels. The book includes probably the oldest account of the fallen angels, the Watchers. They plead with Enoch to intercede for them with God, and he is taken up to heaven. He enters the divine mansion, guarded by cherubim, and an inner hall "of tongues of fire" where God is enthroned, surrounded by millions of angels (1 Enoch 15). God tells

RIGHT: **Enoch, from a detail of the** *Creation Window* **1861, by George Campfield, in All Saints Church, Selsey, Gloucestershire, England.**

Enoch that the fallen angels' plea is in vain, for they "will have no peace".

Archangels, "the ones like flaming fire", then take Enoch on a tour of the cosmos, including the Tree of Life and the place where the Watchers are punished. Enoch names his guides: Uriel (or Suruel), Raphael, Raguel, Michael, Sarakael, Gabriel and Remiel (1 Enoch 20). Raguel is described as the avenging angel and Gabriel as the overseer of the garden of Eden and the cherubim. Michael is later called the "chief" of the angels, and Raphael the angel of healing. Other named angels include Zutuel and Phanuel. Angel guides take Enoch on further journeys to the highest heavens and remoter parts of the universe. He acquires an unparalleled knowledge of God's creation and the angelic realm, and receives visions of the future and the throne of judgment. He returns to earth to write down what he has seen before he is finally taken up to heaven and placed by God "among the angels" (1 Enoch 106).

EARLY MYSTICS AND SAINTS

Throughout the ages, Christian mystics and saints have frequently cited the angels as their source of divine inspiration and vision.

Angels have appeared to saints and mystics since the earliest days of the Church. In the Acts of the Apostles alone, angels appear to Saints Peter and John in prison, to St Philip, to Peter in prison again, and to St Paul when he was imprisoned (Acts 5, 8, 12 and 27). An angel gave St John his visions in the Book of Revelation.

Some saints received their calling through angelic visions. St Cuthbert (*c.*635–682CE) began life as a shepherd boy. One day, when he was 16, he was watching his sheep near Melrose, a famous abbey in the north of England, when he had a vision of angels carrying the soul of St Aidan to heaven. The vision inspired Cuthbert to join Melrose Abbey. He went on to become Bishop of Lindisfarne and one of the most prominent churchmen of his time.

One of the greatest mystics of the Middle Ages was Hildegard of Bingen (1098–1179), the German abbess who was so revered for her wisdom and visionary experiences that she is often called "St Hildegard" despite never having been canonized. She received visions throughout her life, and recounted 26 of them in a work known as *Scivias* (short for *Scito vias Domini*, "Know the ways of the Lord"). In the first vision of Book 1, Hildegard sees God enthroned as an "angel of great counsel" on an iron mountain, which represents his eternal kingdom. In the next vision, Hildegard depicts the fall of Lucifer and his rebel angels, who are represented as "living lamps" or stars.

But it is in her sixth vision that Hildegard has her most brilliant experience of angels.

Christian tradition ranked the angels in nine orders, arranged in three groups of three: angels, archangels and virtues; powers, principalities and dominions; and, at the top, thrones, cherubim and seraphim (see pages 74–93).

Hildegard's vision, though, divides the orders into groups of two, five and two, and sees human nature reflected in the angelic hierarchy. Angels and archangels represent the body and soul, while the cherubim and seraphim symbolize

RIGHT: St Francis receiving the stigmata, from a panel (detail) by Giotto (1267–1337).
LEFT: St Francis feeding the birds, panel (detail) by Giotto (1267–1337).

the knowledge and love of God respectively. The five middle orders represent the five senses.

Hildegard says that she saw the choirs of angels as "armies arrayed like a crown", and illustrated this vision with her own painting. Resembling a mandala, it depicts the angels in nine concentric circles around an empty space that represents the Divine Presence.

One of the most remarkable visitations of angels happened to St Francis of Assisi (*c*.1182–1226), the founder of the Franciscan order. In August 1224, Francis retired with three companions to fast on Mount La Verna, not far from Assisi. During this retreat, on or about the feast of the

Exaltation of the Cross (September 14), Francis went to pray on the mountainside and saw, according to Brother Leo, one of his companions, the extraordinary vision of "a seraph with six fiery wings descend from the height of heaven". As the seraph came near, Francis saw between its wings an image of the crucifixion, and he received the stigmata, the marks of the five wounds of the crucified Christ. According to a vision received by another brother, Matthew de Castiglione, 36 years after the saint's death, Francis appeared and told him that "he who appeared to me was no angel but Jesus Christ himself under the appearance of a seraph, who with his own hands impressed those wounds upon my body."

Another famous recipient of angelic guidance was St Joan of Arc (1412–31). Born into a peasant family, she began to hear her

LEFT: *Joan of Arc*, by Dante Gabriel Rosetti (1828–82). This panel was the last painting upon which the artist worked, finished a few days before his death on April 9, 1882.

"voices" or "counsel" at the age of 13. To begin with, it appears to have been literally a voice, accompanied by a great light. Later on, Joan apparently made out the figures of Michael and other angels, as well as St Margaret and St Catherine. But she rarely spoke about what she saw, and at her trial refused to describe the saints and angels beyond declaring that " I saw them with these eyes, just as I see you."

In 1428 the voices urged Joan to go to the aid of the French king, Charles VII, against the English, and even told her of a sword hidden behind a church altar at Chinon.

Just as her voices had told her she would, Joan ended the English siege of Orléans in 1429. In 1430, however, she was taken prisoner by the English and their allies, who put her on trial for witchcraft and heresy. She was burnt at the stake in May 1431, declaring to the last, according to the official trial record, "that her voices came from God". Many people who had known Joan agreed with her, and in 1455 the Church officially annulled her controversial sentence. Joan was canonized in 1920.

ST TERESA OF AVILA

One of the most revered and respected women of her time, St Teresa of Avila is renowned for her extraordinary mystical experiences.

Born at Avila in Spain, Teresa (1515–82) entered a Carmelite convent in 1535 and soon began to have the mystical experiences that were to make her famous and that ultimately contributed to her canonization. The discipline at her convent was rather loose, and male visitors were allowed. On one occasion Teresa heard a voice declare to her, "I will not have you converse with men, but with angels."

At first people doubted the authenticity of her experiences. One confessor even ordered her to make the sign of the cross when she saw a vision, as if it were an evil spirit. Teresa dutifully obeyed, but in her autobiography she recorded that by then it had become impossible to doubt that her visions were from God.

Other churchmen, however, were impressed by her piety, and it was not long after this that Teresa had perhaps her most extraordinary angelic vision, the "Transverberation", or piercing of her heart by the love of God. She describes the experience in her own typically direct style:

"I would see beside me, on my left hand, an angel in bodily form – a type of vision which I do not usually see, except very rarely. Though I often see representations of angels, my visions of them are of the [mental] type. It pleased the Lord that I should see this angel in the following way. He was not tall, but short, and very beautiful, his face so fiery that he appeared to be one of the highest types of angel who seem to be all burning. They must be those who are called cherubim: they do not tell me their names but I am well aware that there is a great difference between certain angels and others, and between these and others still, of a kind that I could not possibly explain. In his hands I saw a long golden spear and at the end of the iron tip I seemed to see a point of fire. With this he seemed to pierce my heart several times so that it penetrated to my very innards. When he drew it out, I thought he was drawing them out with it, and he left me entirely burning with a great love of God. So sharp was the pain that it made me utter several moans; and so excessive was the sweetness that this intense pain caused me that one can never wish to lose it, nor will one's soul be content with anything less than God. It is not bodily pain, but spiritual."

Teresa was also acclaimed for her remarkable career as a churchwoman. For years she struggled against opposition to her calls for the reform of her own order, the Carmelites, whose discipline she felt was in need of tightening. In the end, Teresa founded a new order, the Discalced (Shoeless) Carmelites, so called because the nuns wore simple habits and sandals rather than shoes.

ABOVE: **The famous marble sculpture, *The Ecstasy of St Teresa* (1647–52), by Giovanni Lorenzo Bernini (1598–1680) fully captures the drama of Teresa's extraordinary vision.**

EMANUEL SWEDENBORG

Swedenborg developed a radical vision of the angelic world in which he understood angels as highly evolved versions of human beings.

The son of a bishop, Emanuel Swedenborg (1688–1772) followed a distinguished career in his native Sweden as a scientist, scholar and administrator. Then one night, at the age of 56, Swedenborg had an extraordinary life-changing dream in which he was carried to the higher realms of the cosmos. From this time on, Swedenborg often experienced visions, trances and mystical dreams, and communicated directly, he claimed, with angels. He resigned his administrative post two years later, in 1747, and was granted a pension from the king of Sweden that enabled him to devote the rest of his life to his spiritual pursuits.

Swedenborg produced a huge number of writings on the relationship between the human and heavenly realms, such as *Heavenly Secrets* (1749) and *Heaven and Hell* (1758). He established his own version of the angelic hierarchy, which he describes in *Heaven and Hell*. Swedenborg believed there were three degrees or levels of angels, each responsible for educating and guiding each other. The closest of the three levels to humans is the "natural" level whereby the angels are freely assisting us in life. At the second level are the "spiritual" angels working in harmony, communicating with one another and teaching the principles of unbounded love. At this level, the angels are closely involved with our evolution and growth. The highest angels are the "celestial" angels. These are closest to God, and live in a state of perpetual purity and goodness.

Swedenborg's central notion is that "people are born to become angels". To Swedenborg, the purpose of creation was to form a heaven of angels that had originally emanated from the human race. He wrote: "If our inner part is

ABOVE: *Angels in Prayer*, by the German artist Caspar David Friedrich (1774–1840), is typical of those paintings in which this artist used a symbolic landscape to express a religious mysticism, not dissimilar to Swedenborg's.

spiritual, we are actually angels in heaven. This means that we are in a community of angels while we are living in our physical body, even if we are not aware of it. After we are released from our physical bodies we associate with angels." He claimed that because angels represented the human race, "there are angels of both sexes in heaven." Angels even married, he said, although their union was not physical but a unification of two minds.

On several occasions Swedenborg visited London, where he died at the age of 84. In 1787, his followers in the city founded the New Jerusalem Church, or New Church, based on his beliefs and experiences. The Church now has followers worldwide.

WILLIAM BLAKE

Throughout his life William Blake claimed to speak with many of the angels and other spiritual beings that feature in his visionary works.

The English artist, poet and visionary William Blake (1757–1827) was born in London, where he lived for most of his life. He became apprenticed as an engraver at the age of 14, by which time, he later wrote, he had already begun to experience visions of angels and other beings. At the age of 10, he told his father that he had seen angels in a tree. These angelic visions were to occur throughout his life. He claimed to have conversations with the angel Gabriel and the Virgin Mary, as well as with ghostly monks, spirits, devils and historical figures.

Blake's view of the angelic realm was influenced by Swedenborg, who lived in London for a time. In *The Marriage of Heaven and Hell* (1790) Blake declares, in a reference to the Resurrection: "And lo! Swedenborg is the Angel sitting at the tomb; his writings are the linen clothes folded up." But Blake also criticized certain aspects of Swedenborg's teachings. For example, Blake did not believe that angels were evolved human beings: for him, the angel was a symbol of the world of spirit, a separate order of creation. Another influence on Blake's concept of angels was the rediscovered Book of Enoch, a copy of which had been brought back from Ethiopia in 1773. Blake illustrated angels from Enoch, as well the prophet himself.

"It is not because angels are holier than men or devils that makes them angels, but because they do not expect holiness from one another, but from God only."

The Marriage of Heaven and Hell

The Marriage of Heaven and Hell is typical of Blake's radical conceptions of the divine and spiritual worlds. In this work, he seeks to unite what he saw as the "active" energy of Hell with the "inactive" passivity of Heaven, seeing angels and devils, or fallen angels, as complementary forces in the universe: "For every thing that lives is Holy." Angel guides feature strongly in *The Marriage of Heaven and Hell* and in Blake's other prophetic books, such as *The Book of Thel* (1789), *America* (1793) and *The Book of Urizen* (1794). In these writings, Blake expressed his lifelong concern with the struggle of the creative spirit to free its natural energies, as well as his compassion for human suffering: "Then cherish pity", Blake wrote, "lest you drive an angel from your door."

BELOW: Blake's drawing, *An Angel Striding among the Stars*, conveys all the power and dynamism of the heavenly beings that the artist so frequently saw in his visions.

THE SENTIMENTAL ANGEL

*In the 19th century angels became popular symbols of sentimental love —
gentle guardians rather than mighty agents of God's power.*

In 19th-century Europe and America there was no decline in the general belief in angels among ordinary Christians, since the existence of angels was, and is, a basic tenet of Christianity – in fact, angels appear even more often in the New Testament than the Old. However, the preceding era of scientific discovery known as the "Age of Reason", or "Enlightenment", had emphasized rational explanations for the cosmos. The idea of studying the angelic realm was taken less seriously by many religious scholars. If angels were studied at all – other than by those in esoteric circles, such as the Swedenborgians – it was usually in a purely biblical context.

But outside scholarly and academic circles, angels acquired a new symbolic popularity in the 19th century as a religious revival went hand in hand with popular Romanticism.

Believing that Reason had done little to improve the general lot of humankind, the Romantics tried to engage more directly with the emotions by appealing to sentiment. Thus angels became increasingly sentimentalized, tending to become the gentle guardians of children, the sick and the unfortunate, rather than awesome agents of divine power.

Angels were generally depicted in the 19th century much as they had been in the Renaissance and Baroque eras. Like their Baroque predecessors, 19th-century painters and sculptors often showed angels as infants, identical in form to the winged Cupids found in scenes from Classical mythology. The cheerful baby "cherubs", or *putti*, often carried bows and arrows, attributes of Cupid. These were far from the awesome cherubim or majestic lightning-clad messengers of the Bible.

Angels on 18th-century gravestones and tombs had often been represented by a winged cherub's head. Mourners of the 19th century preferred beautifully sculpted full-figure (and sometimes life-sized) angels, of either the cherubic variety or, especially later in the century, "adult" angels of the sort that adorn the great 19th-century cemeteries of London and Paris. An angel with drooping wings leaning over the grave was both decorative and symbolic, signifying that the deceased's exemplary Christian life had earned them a place in heaven, and so comforting the bereaved with a reminder that their loved one was in a better place.

Angels were particularly popular on the graves of children, in an age when infant mortality was high and affected almost every family. This also reflected the sentimental popularity of the scene in the Bible where Jesus beckons the children to him, and his words in Matthew 18.10: "Take care that you do not despise one of these little ones; for, I tell you, their angels continually see the face of my Father in heaven."

ABOVE: *Beneath an Angel's Wing*, **by William Strutt (1825–1915), is typical of 19th-century depictions of angels as the guardians of children.**

19TH- AND 20TH-CENTURY ENCOUNTERS

In the course of the 19th and early 20th centuries angelic sightings and visions were reported in places as far apart as America and China, and even on the battlefields of the First World War.

In 1823, at Palmyra in New York State, the 18-year-old Joseph Smith described his vision of an angel called Moroni. The angel told him that a lost tribe of Israel had migrated to America and had buried the golden Tablets of the Law there. Moroni guided Smith to a hill in Massachusetts, where he found the tablets, and told him to found a church based on their teachings. The tablets were translated as the *Book of Mormon* (1830) and the new church eventually settled in Utah.

LEFT: *Why Seek Ye the Living Among the Dead***, by American illustrator Howard Pyle (1853–1911), who, influenced by the theatre as a young man, sought dramatic impact in his work.**

In 1848, 25-year-old Marietta Davis awoke from a nine-day coma at her home in Berlin, New York State, to declare that her spirit had ascended to heaven and seen a choir of angels and redeemed humans. She had even heard Christ singing. She had visited the "Infant Paradise" where a children's choir sang praises to harp accompaniment.

William Booth (1829–1912), who founded the Salvation Army in 1877, recorded the visit of an angel so beautiful he could hardly describe it, beyond saying that it was "at the same time earthly and celestial" and its face "a sun-lit window through which I could see into the depths of the pure benevolent soul within."

In August 1914, shortly after the outbreak of World War I, a story began to circulate that British troops retreating from Mons in Belgium had been protected by a huge, radiant angel in the sky. According to one eye-witness account, there were "three shapes, one in the centre having what looked like outspread wings, the other two not so large.... They appeared to have a long loose-hanging garment of a golden tint."

Sadhu Sundar Singh (1889–1929), a Sikh convert to Christianity, experienced visits to heaven to be instructed in spiritual truths. An angel told him that people had two bodies, spiritual and physical. Singh wrote: "An angel told me that the body that you see is the soul, or spiritual body, possessed while in the temple of flesh on earth."

From the 1920s until 1949 the American missionary H. A. Baker worked among Chinese orphans at his mission in Kunming, Yunnan Province. During this time the children reported numerous angelic visions, which are recorded in Baker's book *Visions beyond The Veil*.

"The centre figure was much taller than the other two and had shining wings which seemed to protect the lesser figures on either side of him."

Eye-witness account from the Battle of Mons, World War I

THE THEOSOPHISTS

Much of the present-day understanding of angels has been inspired by the Theosophists, seen by many as forerunners of the New Age movement.

The Theosophical Society was founded in India in 1875 by Helena P. Blavatsky and Colonel Henry S. Olcott. "Theosophy" ("Wisdom of God") was based on the ancient wisdom that Blavatsky and Olcot had learned from Eastern teachers and, like the "New Age movement" of recent years, it brought together the beliefs of East and West, in particular Hinduism, Buddhism, and Gnostic Christianity.

Theosophical teachings were developed and gradually disseminated overseas, notably by Annie Besant, Alice Bailey and Geoffrey Hodson who were from England. Bailey (1880–1949) claimed that many of her writings had been

RIGHT: *Head of an Angel* (detail), 1889, by Vincent van Gogh (1853–90), was painted 14 years after the founding of the Theosophical Society.

dictated to her by a celestial being named Djwhal Khul. These teachings held that the "Absolute", or "Infinite", emanates an omnipotent force from which shine seven "sub-rays", or "Ambassadors". Each ray has an intelligent "Power", and an archangel of spiritual light. These seven types of divine energy influence everything within us and in our environment. Three rays are called primary rays, or the "rays of aspect"; the remaining four rays are referred to as the "rays of attribute". The seven rays are one of the fundamental teachings of the Theosophists, expounded by Bailey in her book *The Treatise of the Seven Rays* (1949).

The Theosophists also developed the ideal of a "brotherhood/sisterhood" aimed at bringing humanity into close cooperation with angels. Geoffrey Hodson (1886–1983) wrote of his own angelic experiences, claiming they had shown him how angels communicated not only by telepathy, but also by expanding their hearts like an "opening golden rose". Hodson's writings were accompanied by illustrations of these forces as manifestations of colour and light. He also wrote of a visit from a high-ranking angel named Bethelda, who gave instruction on how to collaborate with a variety of angelic beings, from "elementals" and nature *devas* to the archangels, cherubim and seraphim – all in the service of God and humanity.

THE SEVEN RAYS OF THEOSOPHY

PRIMARY RAYS OF ASPECT

1ST RAY Power, Will or Purpose

2ND RAY Love-Wisdom

3RD RAY Active, Creative Intelligence

RAYS OF ATTRIBUTE

4TH RAY Harmony through Conflict, or Beauty or Art

5TH RAY Concrete Science or Knowledge

6TH RAY Abstract Idealism or Knowledge

7TH RAY Ceremonial Order or Magic or Ritual of Organization

THE NEW AGE

The rising popularity of angels in recent years is a part of the New Age, a name given to the widespread interest in alternative spiritual paths.

The latter part of the 20th century saw a steady decline in traditional religious practice in the West. Over the same period this trend coincided with a rising interest in alternative belief systems, including Eastern mysticism and meditation, holistic and traditional healing, astrology, and angels. In the liberating 1960s, this "alternative" trend received a boost when well-known figures, such as John Lennon and George Harrison of The Beatles, became interested in Eastern philosophy and transcendental meditation, popularizing these movements in Britain and elsewhere in the Western world.

By the 1980s the tendency for people to seek a broader and more eclectic range of sources to inspire their own spiritual journeys had acquired a name: the New Age movement. The New Age is generally understood as a shift toward a greater synthesis of the mind, the body, and the spirit.

From the 1960s and 1970s, writers such as Geoffrey Hodson, with their roots in the Theosophical movement, were finding a renewed public interest in their work on angels. In the present age of global media, the subject of angels has become increasingly popular and many angel-work writers and practitioners are inundated with personal accounts of the angelic encounters of their readers. A large proportion of these writers and practitioners have had life-changing angelic experiences of their own. It is often these experiences which inspired them to become healers, therapists or teachers in this field.

"World Angel Day" has become an annual event that brings together leading angel practitioners from around the world. Its aim is not just to invite people of all cultures and nations to invoke and celebrate angels, but also to work harmoniously alongside them in their mission to heal the planet. So far there are groups celebrating World Angel Day throughout Europe, America, Australia and South Africa.

One of the leading names within New Age angel activity is Dorothy Maclean who, with Eileen and Peter Caddy, founded the renowned Findhorn Foundation Community in Scotland in 1962. Acting on inner guidance from the "landscape angels" and nature spirits, the three friends found that they were able to communicate with the essence of nature which opened into the angelic world. Dorothy named these nature spirits *devas* (Sanskrit for shining ones). Dorothy teaches what has become fundamental to the New Age. Working with angels is about connecting with the sacred, uniting with one's inner being and "putting intelligence into action on the material plain".

RIGHT: **This watercolour, *Angel over Le Besset*, by contemporary artist Michael Chase, reflects the current renewed interest in all things angelic.**

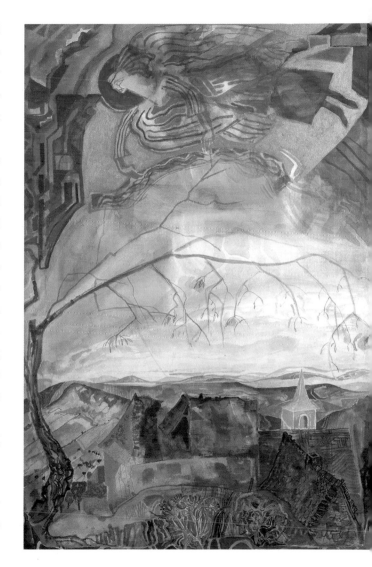

THE ANGELS
IN HEAVEN

✳✳✳✳✳✳✳✳✳✳✳✳✳✳✳✳✳✳✳✳✳✳✳✳✳✳✳✳✳✳

*The number of angels is
traditionally said to be so
enormous as to be uncountable.
Over the centuries theologians
have devised different categories
and ranks within this vast
angelic realm, and have
assigned the angels a whole
repertoire of celestial and
earthly functions.*

LEFT: **Muhammad's Paradise, from** *The History of*
Muhammad, **an 11th-century Persian manuscript,**
shows the angels ranked in the seven heavens.

HEAVENLY HIERARCHIES

To understand the workings of the heavenly realm, religious thinkers have sought to discern an ordered structure within angelic "society".

Anyone today who seeks information about angels could be excused for becoming thoroughly confused by the sheer complexity of the angelic realms and the beings that dwell there. Different authorities give different numbers of heavens and many members of the vast army of angels have interchangeable names and roles. Ancient scriptures, the early Church Fathers and theologians, even art historians — not to mention the doctrines of different faith traditions — all add to the bewilderment, with their conflicting opinions on the truth about angels and the heavenly realm. Added to this historical confusion are the relatively recent reports of people, such as the Theosophist Alice Bailey, who claim to have received detailed accounts of the angelic spheres through meditation and their direct connection with spiritual beings. Today anyone seeking to find out more about angels also has at their disposal a huge quantity of books and websites on angels (with some of which one should exercise a degree of caution).

The Bible offers some hints about the existence of a hierarchy among the angels. Apart from the anonymous angels who deliver important messages from God, there are special beings called cherubim that guard the entrance to Eden and the Ark of the Covenant, as vividly

"All [the angels], as they circle in their orders, look aloft; and downward, with such sway prevail, that all with mutual impulse tend to God."

Dante, The Divine Comedy (1306—21)

ABOVE: **God creating Eve, from the Nuremberg Bible (1483), showing God and the earth, surrounded by a host of angels.**

described in Ezekiel 10. He also describes the great angelic wheels that came to be called "thrones" (see page 51). Isaiah mentions the seraphim, another special type of angel residing close to God's throne. Both Revelation and the apocryphal Book of Tobit mention seven beings that stand before God, generally understood as

archangels — a word not found in the Old Testament and used only twice in the New Testament (Jude 1.9 and 1 Thessalonians 4.16). But other Jewish and Christian writings mention three or even four archangels, while the Judaic Kabbalah cites ten archangels of the Tree of Life. The Qur'an recognizes only four archangels.

Only two angels, Gabriel and Michael, are mentioned by name in the Bible. The name of two more, Raphael and Uriel, are found in the apocryphal books of Tobit and Esdras respectively. Other names, such as Raguel, come from other Jewish writings such as the Book of Enoch. Michael alone is referred to in the New Testament as an archangel (Jude 1.9).

The Book of Daniel suggests that there were angelic "princes", perhaps archangels, assigned to particular lands (Daniel 10). In addition to these special angels the Bible has many ordinary messenger angels, who are only occasionally described in any detail.

The apostle Paul added further names to the list of angelic beings when he described the risen Christ as set at the right hand of God "far above all rule and authority and power and dominion, and above every name that is named, not only in this age, but also in the age to come" (Ephesians 1.21). He also states that "in him all things in heaven and earth were created, things visible and invisible, whether thrones or dominions or rulers or powers – all things have been created through him and for him" (Colossians 1.16).

However, some have argued that St Paul was simply referring to the earthly realm when he spoke of thrones, rulers, powers and dominions (also called dominations), rather than angels or angelic realms; and that the "virtues" he speaks of in some translations of Ephesians 1.21 merely refer to positive moral characteristics. The Church came to accept that Paul was talking about angels, but there was still debate as to how many different types of angel there actually were. Around 200CE Clement of Alexandria proposed that there were seven, which controlled the stars and the four elements of air, earth, fire and water. The first to speak of "the nine choirs of angels" was St Ambrose in the 4th century. Ambrose put forward the orders of seraphim, cherubim, dominions, thrones, principalities, powers, virtues, angels and archangels. But Ambrose's contemporary, St Jerome, again favoured only seven orders: seraphim, cherubim, powers, dominions, thrones, angels and archangels.

Two hundred years later, Pope St Gregory the Great summarized the widely held view: "Almost every page of the Bible tells us that there are angels and archangels, and the books of the prophets tell of cherubim and seraphim. St Paul names [Principalities, Powers, Virtues, Dominions and Thrones]. If we put these two lists together … we get nine orders of angels." Gregory grouped the angels into three groups of three: Seraphim, Cherubim, Thrones; Dominions, Principalities, Powers; and Virtues, Archangels, Angels.

The acceptance of the nine orders was prompted by a book called *Celestial Hierarchies*

RIGHT: **A detail of the musical angels in** *Christ Glorified in the Court of Heaven*, **by Fra Angelico (c.1387–1455).**

78

(*De Coelesti Hierarchia*), which was probably written in the late 5th century. However, the work was long ascribed to a follower of St Paul called Dionysius the Areopagite, a judge in first-century Athens who converted to Christianity after hearing Paul preach (recorded in Acts 17). The supposed author's link with Paul lent the work authority. In later centuries, when the authorship was doubted, the writer was dubbed "Pseudo-Dionysius" (False Dionysius).

Whatever his true identity, Pseudo-Dionysius was a true biblical scholar and was cleary inspired by Paul's letters. *Celestial Hierarchies* claims to be a record of St Paul's vision of heaven, which the apostle described to his new convert. The angelic realms are arranged into nine orders or "choirs" orbiting the throne of God. Pseudo-Dionysius divided them into three groups: Seraphim, Cherubim, Thrones; Dominions, Virtues, Powers; and Principalities, Archangels, Angels. This order differs slightly from the later ordering of Pope Gregory (see page 78).

The author adopted the rabbinic model of the cosmos, in which God is both the centre and the highest point. As the angels surround the Throne of Glory they are ranged into three distinct groups of three, or "triads". These celestial entities

LEFT: *Seated Angels with Orbs in their Hands,* by Ridolfo di Arpo Guariento (*c.*1310–*c.*1370).

radiate outwards from the Source of light and love in a dynamic and ever-moving spiral, the inner (highest) orders transmitting divine energy down the ranks to the outer triad of principalities, archangels and angels, who are nearest to humanity.

This account of the angels was highly influential throughout the Middle Ages. Nevertheless, other versions of the angelic hierarchies continued to appear, listing seven, nine, or twelve orders of angel, including unusual types such as "sanctities", "ardours", "apparitions", "gonfalons", "acclamations" and "warriors". The exact groupings of the orders, and their leaders, were subject to a lively and at times confusing debate.

The confusion was more or less settled, at least in the Christian Church, in the 13th century, when St Thomas Aquinas wrote his *Summa Theologica*. Aquinas accepted Pseudo-Dionysius, adding that the angels included personal guardians for every human being.

Different angelic rankings are found in Judaism and Islam. In Judaism, there are two main lists with ten orders each. The first was proposed by the great rabbi and scholar Moses Maimonides in the 12th century. In descending order it reads: *hayyoth ha-Qadesh* (heavenly creatures); *ophanim*; *erelim*; *hashmalim*; *seraphim*; *malakhim*; *elohim*; *bene elohim*; *cherubim*; *ishim*. It is not easy to translate these names and almost impossible to match them exactly with angels in the Christian hierarchies. The *hamshalim* are often equated with dominions, *ophanim* or *erelim* with thrones, and *malakhim* with virtues. A second list is found in the mystical second-century Jewish work the Zohar, the sacred text of the Kaballah (see page 96): *malakhim*; *erelim*; *seraphim*; *hayyoth*; *ophanim*; *hashmalim*; *elim*; *elohim*; *bene elohim*; *ishim*.

Hints in the Qur'an and in the Hadith (writings about the Prophet) gave rise to the Islamic classification of angels: throne bearers (*hamalat al-'arsh*); cherubim (*karibuyin*); angels of the seven heavens; guardian angels; attendant angels; journeying angels (*sayahun*); and ordinary angels. The Qur'an recognizes four archangels but names only two, Jibril (Gabriel) and Mikha'il (Michael). Islamic tradition names the other two as Azrael and Israfel.

THE TRIADS

Pseudo-Dionysius based his division of the nine choirs on the sacred number three, to produce three triads, or groups of three.

According to Pseudo-Dionysius thoughts emanate from God in the form of pure wisdom and light. This energy travels down the celestial spiral to the angelic triad which is closest to God, which represents God's profound perfection, or, to be more specific, burning love, brilliant light, and perpetual holiness. The energy passes to the second triad, who represent God's sovereignty over creation:

limitless power, irresistible force, and eternal justice. The third triad, closest to the human realm, represents the external actions of God: wise government, sublime revelations, and constant manifestations of divine benevolence.

RIGHT: *The Deity from Whom Proceed the Nine Spheres,* **by William Blake (1757–1827), arranges angels in a hierarchy under God.**

PSEUDO-DIONYSIUS' CELESTIAL HIERARCHY

HIGHEST TRIAD	MIDDLE TRIAD	LOWEST TRIAD
1. Seraphim	4. Dominions (or Dominations)	7. Principalities
2. Cherubim	5. Virtues	8. Archangels
3. Thrones	6. Powers	9. Angels

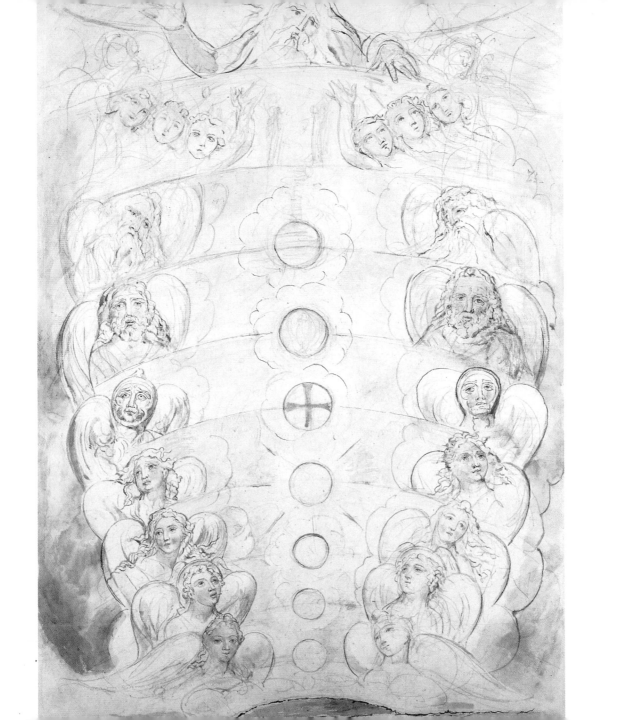

THE FIRST TRIAD

The first, or highest, triad consists of the angels closest to God.
It is made up of seraphim, cherubim and thrones.

Seraphim, or seraphs, are generally accepted as the highest order of God's angelic servants, and their name in Hebrew means "burning ones". They are God's highest servants, directly ministering to him and praising him. The only reference to seraphim in the Bible is in Isaiah 6 where the prophet describes seraphs as having six wings: "With two they covered their faces, with two they covered their feet, and with two they flew." The seraphim stand above the throne of God and call to one another in an endless chant of praise: "Holy, Holy, Holy is the Lord of Hosts; the whole earth is full of His Glory."

RIGHT: Heaven in *The Last Judgment* (detail), by Fra Angelico (*c.*1387–1455). Red is traditionally the colour worn by the seraphim in art.

Cherubim are the first angels to appear in the Bible, posted by God to bar the way to Eden following the expulsion of Adam and Eve (Genesis 3.24). The scriptural image of cherubs is very different from the chubby winged infants they were to become in European art. Their name may derive from the *karibu* of Assyria (see page 26), fierce winged spirits that could have human faces, the bodies of lions or bulls, and eagle-like wings. Cherubim are described in detail in Ezekiel 10 as "four living creatures" with four wings and four faces, supporting the throne of God. Revelation 4.8 says that they have six wings. Images of two cherubim guard the Ark of the Covenant in Exodus 25.

St Augustine said that the cherubim were "the seat of the Glory of God", and St Gregory called them "the fullness of the knowledge of God". In rabbinic and mystic Judaism, cherubim are God's charioteers, and the Zohar describes them as holding up the universe. Christian mystics saw them as the guardians of the fixed stars. Chief among the cherubim are said to be angels called Ophaniel, Rikbiel, and Zophiel.

If the cherubim are the charioteers of God, then the thrones have been described as the actual chariots. Also known as *ophanim* or *galgallim*, which translate as "wheels", thrones are described in the vision of Ezekiel as bright celestial wheels with eyes all around their rims. In Catholic tradition, they occupy the region of transition between the purely spiritual and material worlds. Their chief is said to be an angel variously called Oriphiel, Zabkiel or Zaphiel.

"Their [the thrones'] appearance was like the gleaming of beryl; and the four had the same form, their construction being something like a wheel within a wheel. . . . Their rims were tall and awesome, for the rims of all four were full of eyes all around."

Ezekiel 1.16 & 18

THE SECOND TRIAD

The second, or middle triad is made up of three orders of angels called dominions, virtues and powers.

The chief source for the existence of angels called dominions, virtues and powers is St Paul's letter to the Ephesians (1.21), though he also mentions dominions and powers in his letter to the Colossians (1.16).

Fourth in the celestial hierarchy, dominions are also called "dominations", "angels of dominion" and "lordships". Pseudo-Dionysius refers to them as the "true lords", for this order of angels has the task of regulating the duties of the lower angels and making known the commands of God, which they receive from the seraphim and cherubim.

Dominions ensure that order is maintained in the universe. It is through these angels that God's majesty is manifest, although they appear in physical form to human beings only on rare occasions. In the angelic spiral they are closely related to the seraphim in the triad above them,

reflecting the love of the seraphim on to the principalities, in the lowest triad. Different traditions suggest that the chief of the dominions is an angel variously called either Hashmal or Zadkiel.

The second choir of this second angelic triad, the virtues, occupies the midway point in the angelic hierarchy. Virtues preside over the movement of the sun, moon, stars and other heavenly bodies, and are sometimes known as the "Shining Ones". They are also responsible for weather phenomena such as wind, rain and snow. Virtues are bringers of courage and heroism. The two men "in white robes" who appear to the apostles when Christ ascends to heaven (Acts 1.10) are traditionally said to belong to the order of virtues, as are the guardian angels of children mentioned by Jesus in Matthew 18.10. Michael is sometimes said to be the chief of the virtues as well as the commander of the archangels.

Powers defend the universe and the human race against the agents of evil. They keep watch over the pathways from earth to heaven and ensure that the souls of the dead reach heaven safely. They are therefore also associated with the workings of destiny and fate. Powers are the most ambivalent of all the angelic choirs. Clearly, they were linked with darkness, and in his letter to the Ephesians (6.12) St Paul indicates that they are malevolent. They could be compared with the Egyptian god Seth, a troublesome and much feared deity of chaos and darkness who nevertheless was the only god strong enough to fend off the attacks of evil forces intent on destroying the cosmos. Tradition has it that the powers were the first angels to be created; and that more angels from the ranks of the powers fell (with Lucifer) than from any other of the angelic choirs (see page 103).

The leader of the powers is said to be either Camael or Samma'el (Samael). Both are angels of darkness, especially Samma'el, who appears in some non-biblical scriptures as the angel of

ABOVE: *The Heavenly Militia*, by Ridolfo di Arpo Guariento (*c.*1310–70). It is just such an army of angels that Archangel Michael is believed to lead into battle against the forces of evil.

death, a function sometimes called the "Poison of God". In rabbinical writings Samma'el plays an important role as the chief of the evil angels, while one Christian work, the ninth-century *Apocalypse of Daniel*, names Samma'el as the Antichrist himself.

THE THIRD TRIAD

The third, or lowest triad is the one closest to humanity and comprises principalities, archangels and angels.

In the hierarchy of Pseudo-Dionysius the energy of divine love is strongest in the upper ranks of angels, those closest to the divine Source, and diminishes as it descends down the spiral toward the human realm. Nonetheless, the angels of the lowest triad are still glorious and mighty beings. The energy of the principalities, the leading choir of this triad, is still so great that they cannot be personified in human form, or even imagined on a human scale. These angels oversee the earth as the guardians of nations and cities, and are the protectors of religion. As with the powers in the second triad, St Paul also hints at a darker view of this order when he says that Christ "disarmed the principalities and powers, triumphing over them" in Colossians 2.15.

The nearest angels to humankind, the ones that interact most frequently with our world, are the archangels and angels. Archangels are the chief envoys to earth, the prime intermediaries between God and humankind. Pseudo-Dionysius calls them "messengers that carry divine decrees". The term archangel is somewhat ambiguous, because while they appear relatively low in the

ABOVE: *The Virgin and Child with St John the Baptist and the Three Archangels: Raphael, Gabriel and Michael,* **by Sebastiano Mainardi (1460–1513).**

overall hierarchy, they are also considered among "the chief princes", angels with a particularly close relationship to the divine. The "seven angels who stand before God" (Revelation 8.2) are usually understood to be the seven archangels, who are named by Pseudo-Dionysius as Michael, Gabriel, Raphael, Uriel, Chamuel, Jophiel, and Zadkiel. (These are the archangels we shall be working with in Part 2.) Other sources give as many as twelve or as few as four. Michael, is chief of the order of archangels, but some sources also name him as the chief of the order of virtues. The angels called powers fight evil in the world, but Michael is the commander of the heavenly host, "leader of the sons of light". In Jewish tradition he is the "viceroy of heaven".

"Ordinary" angels are the closest of all to earth and are the intermediaries between the human and the angelic worlds. They attend closely to the lives of individual human beings, acting as personal guides and guardians as well as spiritual mentors. Angels protect individuals from the attacks of dark forces and ensure that their prayers are carried to God.

FEELING THE ANGELIC VIBRATION

New Age thinkers have for some time referred to what they call the "vibrational frequencies" possessed by all beings. In order to get in touch with the angelic realm, it is said, we must attune our own slower human energy "vibrations" to the more refined and higher frequencies of the angels — rather like tuning in to a radio station. Within the angelic hierarchy the celestial beings of the first and highest triad, the seraphs, are said to have the highest angelic vibrational frequency, as they contain the pure creative force of God. The cherubs have a slightly lower level of vibration, and so on down the hierarchy. The thrones, or ophanim, are said to inhabit the region of the heavens where things begin to evolve material form.

Interestingly, quantum physics has proved that all forms of existence — in fact, all atoms — do indeed have a measurable vibrational frequency. This has recently been shown to apply not only to visible physical forms but also to energetic forms which are invisible to the human eye. Could science perhaps still prove the existence of the spiritual world?

ANGELS OF THE ZODIAC

Presiding over every person's birth there are angels of the zodiac, season, month, day, and even the very hour.

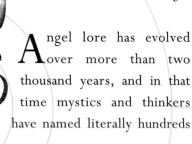

Angel lore has evolved over more than two thousand years, and in that time mystics and thinkers have named literally hundreds of angels. Not only have angels been classified into hierarchies, but individual angels have been given particular functions. By medieval times governing angels had already been identified and named for each hour of the day, each day of the week, each month of the year and each of the four seasons. There were angels, too, for the seven major heavenly bodies (see chart, left) – even each of the moon's 28 phases had its own angel. In many cases, angelic governors were substituted for the pagan gods and goddesses who had previously ruled these natural phenomena. Thus Michael replaced the god Mercury (Hermes) as the angel of the planet Mercury and of Wednesday.

The First Book of Enoch says that God gave the archangel Uriel command over the movements of all the planets and stars, and it was natural that from an early period angels

---

ARCHANGELS OF THE HEAVENLY BODIES

SUN: Raphael

MERCURY: Michael

VENUS: Aniel/Haniel

MOON: Gabriel

MARS: Samma'el, Chamael/Chamuel

JUPITER: Zadkiel

SATURN: Kaphziel/Zaphiel

ANGELIC ZODIAC CHART

Each sign of the zodiac is ruled by an archangel that is considered an archetype of the characteristics of all those born under their sign. In the table below, the archangels are listed alongside the essential activity or state of being with which they are associated. There are variations in the names of the zodiac angels, according to different sources. For example, the angel of Aries is sometimes given as Malahidael and those of Capricorn and Aquarius as Hanael and Gabriel.

ASTROLOGICAL SIGN	CALENDAR PERIOD	ARCHANGEL	ARCHETYPE
Aries	March 21 – April 20	Saraquel	I am
Taurus	April 21 – May 20	Ashmodel	I become
Gemini	May 21 – June 20	Ambriel	I circulate
Cancer	June 21 – July 21	Cael	I create
Leo	July 22 – August 21	Zerachiel	I rule
Virgo	August 22 – September 21	Vael	I provide
Libra	September 22 – October 22	Zuriel	I soothe
Scorpio	October 23 – November 21	Barbiel	I heal
Sagittarius	November 22 – December 20	Adnachiel	I encourage
Capricorn	December 21 – January 19	Orphiel	I order
Aquarius	January 21 – February 18	Cambiel	I power
Pisces	February 19 – March 20	Barchiel	I love

would come to be associated with astrology. Each of the 12 individual zodiac signs is said to have an angel presiding over it, and these are given in the chart on page 91.

On the day a person is born, a considerable number of different angels are said to be active. Just as the moon has a presiding angel and 28 "sub"-angels for each phase, the archangels of the zodiac each have six "sub"-angels to oversee a particular five- or six-day period. Each of these 72 angels embodies qualities associated with its particular time of the zodiacal month.

For example, under the archangel of Capricorn, Orphiel (or Hanael), there are said to be angels named Mebahiah, Poiel, Nemahiah, Ieilael, Harahel and Mitzrael. Someone born between December 22 and 26, at the beginning of Capricorn, comes under the influence of Mebahiah, who is said to promote a strong moral and religious sense and assist those who may wish to have children. If you are born between January 11 and 15, toward the end of Capricorn, the presiding angel is Harahel, who is said to promote receptiveness to new knowledge and ideas.

In addition, each calendar month has its own angel (see chart opposite), so a Capricorn born in December would also be under the influence of Hanael (who is also a month-angel), while January Capricorns come under Gabriel.

It can become even more complex, because there are also archangels of the days of the week: Gabriel (Monday), Khamael (Tuesday), Michael (Wednesday), Tzaphiel (Thursday), Hanael (Friday), Tzaphiel again (Saturday), and Raphael (Sunday). Each archangel apart from Gabriel also serves as the deputy of another: so on Wednesday Raphael is Michael's deputy, and on Sunday it is the other way round, and so on. One of the seven angels also presides over each hour of the day and night.

Added to all this, each zodiac sign is associated with one of the four elements (earth air, fire and water), which also have their own angels, respectively the multi-roled archangels Uriel or Auriel, Raphael, Michael and Gabriel. There are angels, too, for each of the four seasons, respectively Spugliguel (spring), Torquaret (summer), Tubiel (autumn) and Attarib (winter).

ARCHANGELS OF THE MONTHS OF THE YEAR

The archangels of the months are given in the chart below. You will notice that the archangels listed here do not correspond exactly to the ones that appear in the chart on page 91, since the calendar months run over two zodiac signs. Numerous alternative systems have evolved over the centuries, reflecting the fact that angels are capable of many things and of being in many places at the same time.

MONTH	ARCHANGEL	ASTROLOGICAL SIGN
January	Gabriel	Capricorn/Aquarius
February	Barchiel	Aquarius/Pisces
March	Malchidiel	Pisces/Aries
April	Asmodel	Aries/Taurus
May	Amriel	Taurus/Gemini
June	Muriel	Gemini/Cancer
July	Verchiel	Cancer/Leo
August	Hamaliel	Leo/Virgo
September	Zuriel or Uriel	Virgo/Libra
October	Barbiel	Libra/Scorpio
November	Adnachiel or Advchiel	Scorpio/Sagittarius
December	Hanael or Anael	Sagittarius/Capricorn

ANGELS OF
THE TREE OF LIFE

✳✳✳

The visions of the biblical prophets inspired a great Jewish tradition of speculation about the nature of angels, their relationship to God and humankind, and their celestial dwellings. Investigations by mystics of the Merkabah and Kabbalah traditions continue to fascinate today's seekers of esoteric angel knowledge.

LEFT: **This 16th-century French depiction of the** *Tree of the Knowledge of Good and Evil* **(artist unknown) has angels and devilish figures presiding over their respective sides of the tree.**

ANGELS OF THE MERKABAH AND KABBALAH

Jewish mystics believed that with angelic help and the correct esoteric knowledge it was possible to ascend to the presence of God. This idea reached its most elaborate expression in the Tree of Life of the Kabbalah.

The Merkabah is, literally, the glorious Throne-Chariot of God. Merkabah mysticism was inspired by the visions of Ezekiel and other biblical prophets and also by the traditions of Enoch, a great prophet who was taken up to heaven. One of the key aspects of the Merkabah mystic tradition was its special focus on the angels who perpetually surround God's throne and sing his praise:

"The cherubim prostrate themselves before Him and bless. As they rise, a whispered divine voice is heard, and there is a roar of praise. When they drop their wings, there is a whispered divine voice. The cherubim bless the image of the Throne-Chariot above the firmament, and they praise the majesty of the luminous firmament beneath His seat of glory. When the wheels advance, angels of holiness come and go. From between His glorious wheels, there is, as it were, a fiery vision of most holy spirits.... The whispered voice of blessing accompanies the roar of their advance, and they praise the Holy One on their way of return."

Song for the Twelfth Sabbath,
from the Dead Sea Scrolls.

Merkabah mystics claimed that the soul was of heavenly origin and that it was possible for the living to make an ascent to heaven to see the Merkabah and join the angels who worship at it.

The mystics kept their most esoteric knowledge a close secret, but there is a large body of writings arising from the tradition. These include songs said to be sung by the angels before the Merkabah on the Sabbath, which were discovered among the Dead Sea Scrolls. The scrolls belonged to an ancient religious community who lived at Qumran in the Judean desert, near the Dead Sea. During the Jewish War against the Romans in 66–70CE, the community hid its sacred scrolls in nearby caves, where they were discovered undisturbed from the late 1940s onwards.

The Qumran community is today widely identified with the Essenes, a strict Jewish sect who lived in the Judean desert around the time of Christ. The scrolls show that Merkabah speculation was an important part of Essene spirituality. The Essenes regarded themselves as the true Israel, God's elect, already united on earth with the angels in heaven. Every act of praise or worship at Qumran was performed simultaneously by the angels in heaven before the Merkabah. The Essenes were the "children of righteousness" and walked in the spirit of

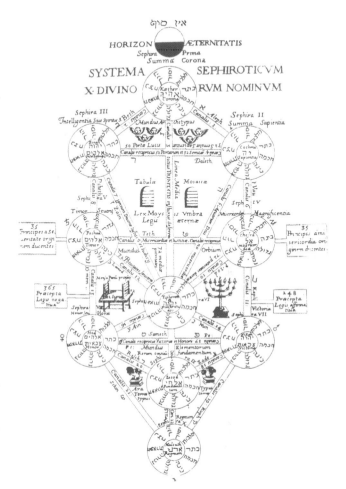

ABOVE: **The Sefirotic Tree of Life of the Kabbalistic tradition from** *Oedipus Aegyptiacus* **(1562) by Athanasius Kirchner, shows a path toward God, with each of the ten stages overseen by an archangel (see pages 100-1).**

DAILY INVOCATIONS OF THE MODERN ESSENES

A revival of Essenism in the 20th century was pioneered by the late Professor Bordeaux Szekely, founder of the Biogenic Society. Present-day Essene devotion includes the following twice-daily invocations of the "seven angels of the Heavenly Father", who oversee the night at sunset, and the "seven angels of the Earthly Mother", who oversee the day at dawn.

SATURDAY AM The Earthly Mother and I are one, she gives the food of life to my whole body.

SATURDAY PM Angel of Eternal Life, descend upon me and give Eternal Life to my spirit.

SUNDAY AM Angel of Earth, enter my physical being and regenerate my whole body.

SUNDAY PM Angel of Creative Work, descend upon humanity and give abundance to all mankind.

MONDAY AM Angel of Life, enter my limbs and give strength to my whole body.

MONDAY PM Peace, Peace, Peace, Angel of Peace, be always everywhere.

TUESDAY AM Angel of Joy, descend upon earth and give beauty to all beings.

TUESDAY PM Angel of Power, descend upon my acting body and direct all my acts.

WEDNESDAY AM Angel of Sun, enter my solar centre and give the fire of life to my whole body.

WEDNESDAY PM Angel of Love, descend upon my Feeling Body and purify all my feelings.

THURSDAY AM Angel of Water enter my blood and give the water of life to my whole body.

THURSDAY PM Angel of Wisdom, descend upon my thinking body and enlighten all my thoughts.

FRIDAY AM Angel of Air, enter my lungs and give the air of life to my whole body.

FRIDAY PM The Heavenly Father and I are one.

light, governed by the archangel Michael, the Prince of Light and Angel of Truth. Everyone outside the sect walked in the spirit of darkness, ruled by Satan, also called Belial. As if to show their purity, Essenes wore robes of pure white.

Another important Merkabah text is the Third Book of Enoch (c. 500CE). This claims to be an account by a famous second-century rabbi, Ishmael, of his journey to heaven. Rabbi Ishmael passes through six celestial palaces, one inside the other. In the seventh palace, which is guarded by angels, the archangel Metatron presents Ishmael before the Merkabah of God. He allows the rabbi to join the angels in singing the Kedushah, the song of praise beginning "Holy, Holy, Holy" in Isaiah 6.

ABOVE: This Dutch medallion shows two angels guarding the Tree of Life.

Metatron then reveals to Ishmael that he is Enoch, who was taken to heaven by God and raised above all the angels. Metatron explains how and why God took him to heaven, and the stages by which he changed into an angel.

Metatron then tells Ishmael about the hierarchies of angels, including the seven archangels in charge of the seven heavens, and the angels within the heavens.

Merkabah mysticism inspired the Jewish mystical tradition known as Kabbalah. The most influential book of Kabbalah was the Zohar, probably compiled by a Spanish mystic called Moses de Léon (d.1305). The Zohar includes esoteric lore on the angels and frequently mentions "the Book of Enoch" – meaning the Third Book of Enoch – and the angel Metatron, the transformed Enoch. Kabbalist teaching is symbolized in the Tree of Life, an image drawn from Genesis 2.9 and 3.22–24. The tree can be found as a symbol linking the earthly and heavenly realms in many other cultures.

The Kabbalistic Tree of Life (see page 99) is both a diagram of creation and a "map" for the initiate's spiritual journey to see the glory of God. The tree represents the different states of consciousness through which the initiate passes on the journey, with ten numbered "stations" called Sefirot (singular: Sefirah), each an aspect of God and each having a corresponding guiding angel. Visiting each Sefirah involves reaching an understanding of each of these aspects of the nature of God. The Sefirot represent the successive emanations from God that constitute the created universe; the emanation that is weakest and furthest from the Source is the material world of humans. Above the tree is Ein Soph, the unknowable central mystery of God, who permeates the Sefirot with his light.

Ein Soph first emanates Keter, the Crown, the creative force of divine love and the Sefirah at the top of the tree. This then radiates down through the intervening Sefirot via 22 interconnecting pathways to the lowest Sefirah, the Kingdom (Malkut), which represents the material world of human consciousness.

Each of the ten Sefirot, also called "gates of light", is overseen by an archangel, except Keter and Malkut, which each have two angelic rulers, making 12 archangels in all. The archangels Metatron and Shekinah oversee Keter at the very top. Metatron, the vice-regent of God, represents human consciousness transformed, and Shekinah is the embodiment of the divine presence in creation. Sandalphon and Auriel watch over Malkut at the bottom, the entrance to the tree, and protect the embarking initiate from evil.

All angels are said to derive from one or other of the Sefirot, and they are grouped into "camps" led by one of the archangels in accordance with the Sefirah from which they come. Hence, the archangel Michael and his "camp" derive from the Sefirah of Geburah, and the archangel Gabriel and his "camp" derive from the Sefirah of Hod, and so on.

THE SEFIROT AND THE ANGELS OF LIGHT

The ten Sefirot of the Kabbalah are arranged in an interconnected hierarchy represented as a "Tree of Life".

Each Sefirah has a mystical name that represents an aspect of the divine being, and is overseen by

an angelic order or "camp" led by one or two archangels that embody the principles of their Sefirah.

The names of the ten camps are given in the Zohar.

SEFIRAH	MEANING	ORDER	ANGEL
Keter	Crown	Malakhim	**METATRON:** The Powerful, and **SHEKINAH:** The Bride of Heaven
Chokmah	Wisdom	Erelim	**ZAPHKIEL:** The Compassionate
Binah	Understanding	Seraphim	**RAZIEL:** The Wise
Chesed	Mercy	Hayyoth	**SAMAEL:** The Administrator
Geburah	Justice	Ophanim	**MICHAEL:** The Leader
Tifaret	Beauty	Hashmalim	**ZADKIEL:** The Comforter
Netzach	Victory	Elim	**RAPHAEL:** The Healer
Hod	Splendour	Elohim	**GABRIEL:** The Messenger
Yesod	Foundation	Bene Elohim	**HANAEL:** The Warrior
Malkut	Kingdom	Ishim	**SANDALPHON:** The Guardian, and **AURIEL:** The Companion

FALLEN ANGELS

✦✦✦✦✦✦✦✦✦✦✦✦✦✦✦✦✦✦✦✦✦✦✦✦✦✦✦✦✦✦✦

For early Jewish and Christian writers the existence of a host of angels who had rebelled against God helped to explain why there was evil in the world. For their transgression — most commonly held to be the sin of pride — these angels had been cast out of heaven, together with their leader, Satan.

LEFT: The fall of the angels from the orderly ranks of heaven to the fiery chaos of hell is dramatically conveyed in this 15th-century French painting (artist unknown).

THE HOSTS OF SATAN

A few enigmatic passages of the Old Testament inspired the story that a group of evil angels had fallen from the heavens, never to return.

Genesis 6 tells how "sons of God" married human women and apparently bred a race of "mighty men" called Nephilim, which means "fallen ones" in Hebrew. Directly following this story, though not explicitly linked to it, is the account of how God sent the Flood to destroy wicked humankind.

The earliest known account of the fall of the angels, in chapters 6–11 of the First Book of Enoch (second century BCE), expands the Nephilim story. Led by Semyaz, the "sons of God" are angels that descend from heaven, driven by lust for mortal women and a sinful desire to reproduce (sinful because only God can create angels). But their offspring are monstrous giants who devastate the world and began to devour the people. The fallen angels, also called the "Watchers", under a senior angel called Azazel, teach humans forbidden "eternal secrets" such as how to make weapons, perform magic and adorn themselves. (In contrast, other writings say that the first humans learnt beneficent arts, such as agriculture, from the archangel Michael.) As a result God orders Michael, Raphael and Gabriel to bind the Watchers under the earth until Judgment Day, and to destroy their offspring.

In this version of the angels' fall, Semyaz does not initiate their sin. But other accounts place responsibility firmly on the ringleader of the errant angels, who is said to be guilty of the sins of pride and arrogance. The main source for this idea is Isaiah 14.12–15:

RIGHT: *The Fall of the Rebel Angels*, by Sebastiano Ricci (1658–1734), powerfully depicts the archangel Michael, with his sword and shield, ejecting the rebel angels from heaven.

"How you are fallen from heaven
O Day Star, son of Dawn!
How you are cut down to the ground,
You who laid the nations low!
You said in your heart,
'I will ascend to heaven,
I will raise my throne
Above the stars of God
I will make myself like the Most High'
But you are brought down to Sheol,
to the uttermost parts of the pit."

Isaiah 14.4 addresses this to "the king of Babylon", probably meaning a real earthly ruler, Israel's enemy. But by Christian times "Day Star", or Lucifer (Lightbearer) in Latin, was taken as the name of the chief fallen angel. A similar passage in Ezekiel 28 addressed to "the Prince of Tyre" was understood in much the same way.

Two traditions arose from this. In one, God had created Adam truly "in his image" as a glorious superhuman being. God commanded the angels to worship Adam, but Satan and his followers refused because, as Satan himself says in an anonymous 1st-century work called *The Life of Adam and Eve*: "I am prior to him in creation; before he was made I was already made. He ought to worship *me*." For this arrogance Satan and his fellows are "cast onto the earth". A similar account appears several times in the Qur'an, where Satan (Iblis or Shaytan) refuses to bow to Adam on the grounds that angels were created of fire but Adam only of clay (Sura 7).

In the other tradition, Satan and the rebel angels tried to set up a rival throne to God's. In the Second Book of Enoch, parts of which may date to the 1st century, God tells Enoch that following the creation of the angels on the second day, one of the archangels thought "that he could place his throne higher than the clouds which are above the earth, and that he might become equal to my power. And I hurled him out from the height, together with his angels."

Like the good angels, the fallen angels have a hierarchy, under a leader called Satan (among other names). Some other evil angels are also named. In 1 Enoch there are 18 senior fallen angels, including Azazel, Amasras, Baraqiyel and

RIGHT: *Satan Addressing his Potentates, c.1816–18,* a William Blake illustration in an edition of John Milton's *Paradise Regained* (1671).

Kokabel. Some have special roles: Azazel taught humans the arts of war and vanity, and Amasras taught spells "and the cutting of roots" (the knowledge of poisonous or medicinal potions made from plants). Medieval thinkers evolved a hierarchy of archdemons to parallel the seven archangels in heaven. Each archdemon oversaw a deadly sin: Lucifer (Pride); Mammon (Avarice); Satan (Anger); Asmodeus (Lechery); Beelzebub (Gluttony); Leviathan (Envy); and Belphegor (Sloth).

The fallen angels were said to live either on the earth, or imprisoned under it, or even within the heavens, where they underwent perpetual punishment. Because evil still existed in the world, it was assumed that some angels had escaped God's initial punishment and the Flood. The Book of Jubilees (second century BCE) says that God allowed Satan to keep a tenth of his followers free as agents of punishment on humanity. But all the ancient writers, including those of the New Testament (Matthew, Jude, Revelation), agreed that the evil angels would meet their final end at the Last Judgment. In Revelation, the destruction of Satan and his angels takes place near the end of time after a mighty battle with the good angels under Michael (Revelation 12.7–9, 20.1–3).

TEMPTER OF HUMANKIND

The leader of the fallen angels goes by many names, including Satan, the Devil, the great dragon, the serpent, Semyaz, Beelzebub and Satanail.

In the 6th century Pope St Gregory the Great said that before his downfall Satan had been the chief of the seraphim and head of the angelic order of virtues. To emphasize how great was his fall, Satan was described almost as God's favourite, and Christian writers took Ezekiel 28 to refer to him: "You were the signet of perfection, full of wisdom and perfect in beauty" (Ezekiel 28.12). Seraphim normally had six wings, but this majestic angel had 12. Satan, said Gregory, wore all the other angels as

✻✻✻✻✻✻✻✻✻✻✻✻✻✻✻✻✻✻✻✻✻✻✻

"The sin, both of men and of angels, was rendered possible by the fact that God gave them free will."

C.S. Lewis (1898—1963)

a garment, "transcending all in glory and knowledge."

In the 13th century, St Thomas Aquinas argued that Satan was not a seraph but a cherub, "as cherubim are derived from knowledge, which is compatible with mortal sin; but seraphim are derived from charity, which is incompatible with mortal sin."

The *Life of Adam and Eve* explains that when Satan fell he took his revenge by tempting God's wonderful creation, Adam, to sin. The fall of Adam and Eve was the source of all human ills, especially death, and Satan came to be seen as the chief agent of human sin and misfortune. However, the evil character of Satan developed only gradually. In Genesis it is a serpent that tempts Eve, and in the Hebrew Bible, Satan is not a name but a description, Hebrew *ha-satan*, "the adversary". The *satan* in Numbers 22.22 is "the angel of the Lord" sent to avert Balaam from wrongdoing. Satan in the Book of Job is neither necessarily evil nor fallen, but does God's bidding by inflicting misfortune upon Job. This "adversary" is part of a cosmos in which seemingly arbitrary suffering has its place as a test of faith for the righteous.

BELOW: **An illustration to Milton's** *Paradise Lost* **(1667)** *– Satan Contemplating Adam and Eve in Paradise* **by John Martin (1789–1854).**

By the 1st century, though, Satan had become the name of a single and unequivocally evil being that was identified with the serpent of Genesis, the chief of the fallen angels, and Beelzebub, the "prince of the demons" in the Gospels. Revelation 12.9 calls him "the great dragon … that ancient serpent, who is called the Devil and Satan, the deceiver of the whole world." Satan controlled the powers of evil. But just as God had originally created him, it was by God that Satan would one day be destroyed.

THE GREAT BELOVED ARCHANGELS

This section focuses on the seven great archangels and the practical ways in which they can guide us in our everyday lives. There are also useful meditations tailored to each specific archangel and designed to help with issues ranging from healing and protection to bringing joy into your life.

LEFT: Vision of the seven angels playing harps, from a late 13th-century French manuscript of the Apocalypse.

CONTACTING ANGELS

Angels may not be at our beck and call, but they are a constant presence in our world, ready to provide guidance when needed. With good meditation practice, an open heart and the right attitude, we can call upon their loving energy to help us and those around us to lead better, more fulfilling lives, both spiritually and practically.

LEFT: **An angel from** *The Coronation of the Virgin,* **c.1488–90 (detail), by Sandro Botticelli, (c.1444–1510).**

MEDITATION AND PRAYER

While working with angels does have some unique aspects, much of the base work is common to meditation and prayer of any form.

The seven archangel meditations (on pages 130–1, 136–7, 142–3, 146–7, 150–1 and 153) are ones that I have used successfully in my workshops on communicating with angels, and have adapted for use in this book. They are based on my own experience and that of my clients, as part of the current growing phenomenon of angelic contact and meditation. As such they are based on practical experience rather than scriptural evidence.

The advice and exercises given are designed to introduce you to working with archangels and their primary energies, and also to help you to grow in your expertise so that you can bring angels into your life in tangible and beneficial ways. I address problems and obstacles that you are likely to encounter in your everyday life and show you how the angels can help you to overcome these.

Always remember, though, that you cannot summon angels at will like servants, and these meditations are not quick-fix solutions. Nor do angels act as "magicians". An angel is not a Santa Claus bearing gifts that correspond to your Christmas wish list.

Angels are ever watchful for when we are in a receptive state of mind. By practising these exercises you will gradually become more open to their messages, love and guidance. They will bring you untold spiritual gifts, some of which you may find challenging.

Remember that petitioning angels for their assistance, talking with them, meditating and asking for their divine wisdom, is not the same as "worshipping". Angels are mediators: they carry your prayers to the Source, then transmit divine guidance back to you. They are messengers between you to God, whoever or whatever you perceive "Him" to be, and back again.

When working closely with angels, you can often sense a great feeling of energetic, protective strength, or gentle, loving compassion surrounding you. This is what is usually meant as the "masculine" or "feminine" energy emitted by an angel's presence, but it does not mean that the angel is specifically male or female. In all aspects of life there are representations of both the masculine and the feminine, the *yin* and the *yang*, the balance of which is vital for wholeness and completion.

One of the first steps in communicating with angels is to create an area or space of harmony where you feel safe and truly at peace. Make sure that it is away from ringing

LEFT and RIGHT: Fresco (details) of angels kneeling in prayer from the side walls of the chapel in the Palazzo Medici-Riccardi, Florence, Italy, by Benozzo di Lese di Sandro Gozzoli (1420–97).

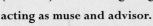

telephones and any noise or distractions. If your space is indoors, play some soft or ethereal music to create a relaxing atmosphere; light a candle to symbolize purity, the fire of creative love and the light of angelic wisdom. If you have any pictures of angels, you may like to put them in this place, with some fresh flowers, again to symbolize the purity and beauty of creation. If you are in a garden, sit quietly where you will be undisturbed, and concentrate on the beauty and fragrance of nature surrounding you.

When you decide to communicate with the angels, your attention and intention are key. Angels are an almost incomprehensibly vast source of love for humanity. Your request must always come from the heart, with gratitude, and be motivated by seeking the best possible outcome for all concerned. (A word of warning: self-centred motives are also heard without judgment, as a promise has been made that your prayers will always be answered, but

RIGHT: *The Inspiration* by Gustave Moreau **(1826–98) is one imagining of a guardian angel acting as muse and advisor.**

the outcome may not be what you expected. An angel cannot change your "karma". Only you can do that.)

When you reach the point in the meditation where you are actively seeking an archangel's

"The guardian angels of life sometimes fly so high as to be beyond our sight, but they are always looking down upon us."

Jean-Paul Richter (1763—1825)

presence, call the archangel's name gently out loud. Your voice adds power to the intention. Do not worry if you do not feel comfortable doing this at first — simply follow your instincts until you become practised.

At the end of your communication, whatever it's purpose or results, always remember to express your gratitude. Thank the angels and the Source of all Creation.

There are as many different ways to meditate as there are people on the planet. Gradually you will come to realize that no one way is the right way or wrong way. Once you have developed a method of relaxing and focusing that works for you, then that is your right way to meditate.

Primarily it is important to be as comfortable as you can be, either seated on the floor or in a chair — you may wish to support yourself with cushions. If you are in discomfort, obviously your attention will wander to the point of irritation and your concentration will be impaired. Some people like to remove their shoes and socks, and keep their feet flat on the floor. This way they remain "grounded" throughout the meditation.

Breathing and relaxation techniques are found in many disciplines such as the numerous forms of Buddhist practice and yoga. While these techniques can provide great benefit, they are not essential to connecting with angels.

Be gentle with yourself. As with any other form of exercise, practice improves the strength of your "spiritual muscles". Even if you find it difficult at first, don't give up. Meditation is so beneficial to your mind, body and soul that you will soon find it becomes easier, and you will inevitably make it part of your daily routine.

OVERLEAF: *The Seven Liberal Arts*, by Giovanni dal Ponte (*c*.1385–1437).

MICHAEL

Michael is arguably the best known of the archangels, and as the archangel of protection his principal quality is that of the holy warrior.

Across the Jewish, Christian and Muslim traditions, Michael is considered the greatest of the archangels. He is the chief protector and warrior, often depicted in classical art in full armour, wielding an unsheathed sword and holding the scales of justice. At the Last Judgment it is Michael who will weigh and balance good deeds against bad.

The image of Michael as the archetypal warrior is believed to have originated with the Chaldeans of Mesopotamia, who worshipped him as a demi-god. In Jewish legend, Michael stands with God besides Gabriel, Raphael and Uriel as one of the mighty four. It was Michael who, as related in the Book of Jude, rescued the

RIGHT: An 18th-century Greek icon of Michael in his typical attire of battle armour, wielding an unsheathed sword.

ARCHANGEL MICHAEL

ARCHANGEL OF PROTECTION

DAY OF THE WEEK: Sunday

ASSOCIATED COLOUR: blue

• The name Michael means "who is as God".

• Chief of archangels and one of the seven who stand in the presence of God. In the angelic hierarchy he is chief of the order of virtues (see pp.86–7).

• The angel of protection, mercy, repentance, righteousness and sanctification.

• Guardian protector of Israel; patron of the Catholic Church and knights during the Middle Ages. Declared patron saint of police in 1950 by Pope Pius XII.

• Provides physical protection for travel, as well as emotional and psychic protection.

In the illuminated manuscript, text boxes read:

archangt̃s michael pug
nar cū dracone idest dyā
bolo ᴣ angeli etus cū
eo.

ſunc facta eſt ſalus et
uirtus ᴣ regnū dei nr̄i
ᴣ potestas xp̄i etus.

ABOVE: **An illumination from the** *Liber Floridus* **(*c*.1120) by Lambert of Saint-Omer, showing the archangel St Michael killing the dragon. Note his shield bearing the familiar red cross of St George, whose own dragon legend first appeared in the fourth century CE.**

body of Moses from Satan's angel Samma'el, after the devil had claimed the body because Moses had murdered an Egyptian. Michael is also one of the four archangels of the Islamic faith, in which he is known as Mikhail.

In the Bible, Michael is exceptional in being seen as head of an angelic army. He argues with the devil (Jude 1.9), and during the war in heaven against Satan conquers the dragon (Revelation 12.7). This feat was later echoed in the fourth-century Greek legend of St George that was made so popular by the troubadours of the 14th century. Michael is first mentioned in the Old Testament in a message to Daniel, and is said to be "one of the chief princes" (Daniel 10.13). It is in the book of the prophet Daniel that we learn that Michael is a special guardian angel to God's people in Israel, protecting them against the threat from Greece and Persia.

The archangel Michael is also of great importance in the angelology of the Dead Sea Scrolls. In one entitled *War of the Sons of Light Against the Sons of Darkness*, Michael is called the "Prince of Light" and leads the battle against the angels of darkness. Further, when the Sons of Light go into battle, they have the names of several of the archangels on their shields, and one of these names is Michael.

In apocalyptic literature and orthodox Christianity, in particular, Michael is shown assisting the Saviour in conquering the forces of darkness and restoring the world to perfection. Similarly, New Age light workers who draw upon the concepts of the *devas*, angels, and the seven rays of Theosophy (see pp.70–1), believe that Michael is currently the most important emissary of God, working closely with the earth during the current transition into the Age of

Aquarius. This will mark the end of an era of patriarchal power, and the beginning of a new age of humanity, equality, compassion and communion. Anyone interested in working with angelic forces, and the "warrior angel" in particular, is responding to the call of Michael.

Michael's protective powers

We can turn the principle of the angelic warrior Michael, carrying the sword of righteousness and slaying the dragon, to practical use by applying it to the destruction of our own inner "demons".

Michael can also be called upon for emotional and psychic protection. This is especially helpful in times of confrontation. Many believers now call upon Michael to protect them against malevolent psychic attack from those with whom they are in conflict.

You can ask the archangel Michael to provide physical protection when you are travelling simply by asking, "Archangel Michael, protect me." At the same time, imagine a blue light of protection surrounding you, your companions and your vehicle or mode of transport.

CUTTING UNWANTED TIES

On our spiritual journey we cannot carry the baggage of pain, guilt, shame and blame with us. We need to set ourselves and others free in order to move into the light. This meditation helps you to cut those ties and start your journey in earnest.

In the furtherance of your spiritual destiny, it is important to sever any negative emotional ties. In this exercise you are asking Michael to cut the bonds binding you to a troubled relationship, an emotional blockage, or some other situation that is holding you back.

The scope of this exercise is far-ranging, and it can be used in many circumstances. It can help you to disconnect from a specific person or people (steps 7–10), let go of a painful memory or negative emotion, or strengthen your resolve in breaking a bad habit or addiction (steps 4–6).

Be prepared to see pictures or symbols, hear words in your head, or simply feel that you "know" what you are being shown (steps 3–4). You may feel a physical pressure somewhere on or within your body, but you do not need to pay attention to it. You will probably find that your emotions are close to the surface once you are finished.

Do not be alarmed if you were unable to cut the ties cleanly or if you did not understand the symbols you were shown – not everyone is ready to let go the first time. Depending on what you are trying to let go of, and how long that connection has existed, you may need to practise the exercise on a regular basis in order to strengthen your detachment incrementally. It is hard to let go of old ties and habits, so it is natural to feel some subconscious reluctance at first. But gradually you will find the visualizations in this exercise easier to do, and long after you have finished you will feel the benefits of knowing that you can move on.

1 Sit comfortably in your meditational space, breathing slowly and deeply.

2 Invite the archangel Michael to come close to you, and visualize him drawing near you.

3 Imagine that you are carrying a bag on your back. Place it on the ground, but with one troublesome strap still attached to you.

4 Ask Michael to show you the bag's contents one by one, and to strengthen your resolve in letting these things go.

5 Ask Michael to cut the strap still attached to your body with his mighty silver sword.

6 Visualize a hole appearing in the ground, and watch the bag disappearing into it. Ask Michael to seal the hole for all time, blessing the site and blessing you.

7 Now picture the person or people who you feel are holding you back.

8 Next visualize a large figure of eight made from rope, surrounded by golden light. Place the person(s) in one half and yourself in the other, at a comfortable distance.

9 Now see Michael's sword cutting through the intersection of the figure of eight. Watch the rope as it frays, thread by thread.

10 Wish the person(s) well on their path, and thank them for allowing you the freedom to continue along your own path unhindered.

11 Thank the archangel Michael for his help, then sit quietly in the presence of your guardian angel for a while. Concentrate on your breathing and gradually bring your attention back to your surroundings.

GABRIEL

In his role as the angel of revelation and the bringer of truth, the archangel Gabriel can guide and encourage you along your true path.

The story told in the diaries of the 18th-century artist William Blake is that, on being commissioned to paint an angel, Blake asked aloud, "Who can paint an angel?" An invisible presence replied, "Michelangelo could." Blake further enquired, "How do you know?" The answer he was given was: "I know for I was there; I sat for him. I am Gabriel."

As we have seen in the first part of this book (see pages 21–47), the archangel Gabriel is found in the traditions of the three major monotheistic faiths. According to both Judaism and Christianity, Gabriel is one of the seven archangels who surround the throne of God.

RIGHT: *The Angel Gabriel*, by Simone Martini (1284–1344). In paintings of Gabriel as the angel of the Annunciation, he is often shown holding a lily as a symbol of the Virgin Mary's purity.

ARCHANGEL GABRIEL

ARCHANGEL OF ANNUNCIATION, GUIDANCE AND RESURRECTION

DAY OF THE WEEK: Wednesday

ASSOCIATED COLOUR: white

• Gabriel's name means "God is my strength".

• The Sumerian root *gbr*, means "governor", but has also been interpreted to mean "power".

• The archangel Gabriel is often depicted with a trumpet, reflecting his role as a messenger of God.

• Practically speaking, the archangel Gabriel provides guidance on spiritual growth and the direction of your future. He can help you to find the clarity to make decisions about your dreams and goals, and the discipline to continue on your chosen path.

He is also one of only two archangels mentioned by name in both the Old and New Testaments (the other being Michael), where he acts primarily as a messenger of God.

Gabriel is perhaps the most cherished angel in the Christian tradition, where he is very much seen as the angel of mercy and is synonymous with redemption. It was Gabriel who announced the births of John the Baptist and Jesus Christ.

The archangel Gabriel appears four times in the Old Testament, first to Daniel (Daniel 8.16 and 9.21 – see pages 52–54). Then he appears to Zechariah as he is burning incense at the altar in

ABOVE: *The Angel of the Annunciation* **from the altarpiece of the Chapel of San Niccolo dei Guidalotti in the Church of San Domenico in Perugia by Fra Angelico (*c.*1387–1455). That an archangel as great as Gabriel is shown kneeling in homage (before Mary) denotes the spiritual perfection of the woman chosen to be the Mother of God.**

the temple – it is Gabriel who announces that Zechariah's wife is to give birth to a son named John (Luke 1.11–19). Lastly, in the familiar story of the Annunciation, it is Gabriel who appears to the Virgin Mary to tell her that she is going to give birth to Jesus, the Messiah and Son of God (Luke 1.26–38).

Mentioned several times in the First Book of Enoch, the archangel Gabriel is very important in non-Biblical Jewish literature as well. According to 1 Enoch 53.6, he is one of four angels – together with Michael, Raphael and Uriel – who will cast Satan (Azazyeel) and his minions "into a furnace of blazing fire, that the Lord of spirits may be avenged of them for their crimes, because they became ministers of Satan, and seduced those who dwell on earth".

In Islamic lore it is Gabriel (Jibral in Islamic texts), the Angel of Truth, who is believed to have appeared to Muhammad and dictated to him the Qur'an verse by verse.

In the Dead Sea Scrolls book *War of the Sons of Light with the Sons of Darkness*, the Sons of Light go into battle with the names of several angels, including that of Gabriel, on their shields.

Gabriel is the ruler of the cherubim and of Paradise. In Milton's *Paradise Lost* (1667) Gabriel is placed at the eastern gate of Paradise as chief of the angelic guards. Satan tricks his way into Paradise where he tempts Adam and Eve, but is then seized by two of Gabriel's angelic scouts and banished from the Garden of Eden.

"*Gabriel, one of the holy angels, who is over Ikisat, over paradise, and over the Cherubim.*"

1 Enoch 20.7

A Female Archangel?

It is interesting that in heaven Gabriel is seated to the left of the throne of God. This position has been interpreted by some thinkers to indicate that Gabriel is the only female archangel in the angelic hierarchy. Further evidence of this strong feminine aspect is Gabriel's role as ruler of the moon. The moon is generally recognized in esoteric terms as symbolic of all things feminine.

Another pointer to the possibility that Gabriel is actually female is that it is always Gabriel who announces important births. Not only does Gabriel herald the births of John the Baptist and Jesus Christ in the New Testament, but also, in apocryphal texts, Gabriel foretells the birth of Samson, and of the Virgin Mary. This quite naturally led to Gabriel being regarded as the angel that presides over childbirth. Other sources claim that the reason Mary was not afraid of the angel who visited her was because she did not assume her visitor to be a man. Gabriel is also said also to be the teacher of wisdom to the incoming soul of the unborn child during its nine-month gestation.

FINDING YOUR SPIRITUAL DIRECTION

Many people feel that they lack direction in their lives. Calling upon the archangel Gabriel to provide guidance toward your true spiritual path can help you to focus on building a better, more rewarding life.

The difference between whatever we imagine to be our "perfect" life and our actual daily reality can sometimes lead to a sense of lethargy, or dissatisfaction with our lives. Gabriel can shed light on your true priorities and guide you in the pursuit of your goals.

Perhaps you are thinking of some sort of change, whether in job, career, or location. Alternatively, you may feel that your life is aimless and that you need to find a sense of purpose — whether practically or spiritually. Gabriel can help you find your path to greater fulfilment. But remember, the focus of this exercise is not pure ambition or material gain.

Be alert to the signs that you have asked for (step 6) — they may appear in the most surprising form. Ask that any messages you receive be clear and comprehensible.

At times when you need guidance, but are unable to perform the full exercise, you can say the following prayer:

"Archangel Gabriel, In the divine light of truth and God's love I ask for your assistance. I am ready to offer myself in service to humanity. Please show me what it is I am required to do.

"Please share with me your wisdom, in the knowledge that I am committed to doing my best. Show me my full potential and help me to fulfil it. So be it. Amen."

1 Sit comfortably on a chair, with your back straight and feet flat on the floor. Rest your hands on your thighs, with your palms turned up in an expression of receiving.

2 Concentrate on your breathing, drawing each breath deeply into your diaphragm before exhaling fully. Relax your entire body with every exhalation, from your scalp and facial muscles down to your toes and fingers.

3 Do not fight your thoughts as they enter your mind. Observe them, then let them drift away as you bring your concentration toward communicating with the archangel Gabriel.

4 Continue breathing deeply, and imagine that you are absorbing a pure white light through the crown of your head. Visualize it being absorbed into every sinew, bone, muscle, organ and cell of your body, and out through the pores of your skin.

5 Ask that this re-energizing light of divine love cleanse, purify and revitalize your heart, mind and soul, suffusing you with a positive commitment to following your true path.

6 Invite Gabriel into this brilliant white light. Ask him for guidance and clarity in the direction of your life and spiritual journey.

7 Allow any thoughts, colours, pictures or words to form in your mind's eye. Remain relaxed, you can analyze them later.

8 Thank Gabriel for his assistance. Become aware of your body once more, and gently open your eyes.

9 Finally recall the thoughts or pictures that came to you, and contemplate what they could be showing you. Keep them in mind and let their meaning and inspiration come to you unforced during the rest of the day.

RAPHAEL

One of the four great archangels alongside Michael, Gabriel and Uriel, Raphael is the great healer and patron of travellers.

In the Book of Tobit, Raphael is the guide and companion of Tobit's son Tobias, and at the end of the journey reveals himself as "one of the seven holy angels" who attends the throne of God. In 1 Enoch (1.40) he is "one of the four presences, set over all diseases and all the wounds of the children of men."

One of the oldest magical texts attributed to King Solomon, *The Testament of Solomon*, (translated by F.C. Conybeare, 1898), tells us that when Solomon prayed to God for help in building the temple in Jerusalem, Raphael brought the Hebrew king a magic ring. This ring was engraved with the pentalpha (five-pointed star) and had the power to control demons.

RIGHT: The archangel Raphael as depicted by a New Mexican folk artist (artist and date unknown).

ARCHANGEL RAPHAEL

ARCHANGEL OF HEALING

DAY OF THE WEEK: Thursday

ASSOCIATED COLOUR: green

• Raphael's name means "God has healed" or "the shining one who heals"; *rapha* in Hebrew means "healer" or "doctor".

• Jewish legend holds that it was Raphael who gave Noah the book of medical cures called the *Sefer Raziel*.

• Raphael helps with issues of wholeness, healing, vision, truth and abundance. He also assists with overcoming disease, degeneration, superstition, error and lack or insufficiency, and healing deep emotional wounds such as those caused within personal relationships.

In this way Solomon was able to complete the building of the Temple using the "slave labour" of the subdued demons.

In 1 Enoch (53.6), Raphael is further named as one of four angels – with Michael, Gabriel and Uriel – that will cast Satan (Azazyeel) and his minions "into a furnace of blazing fire…".

New Age thinkers associate Raphael with the element of air. He can be petitioned to help you with physical, emotional and spiritual healing, and mending rifts in relationships. You can call on Raphael to use you as a channel for God's healing energy – whether on a personal, social, or worldwide scale.

The story of Raphael and Tobias

Tobias's father, Tobit, was a righteous man who had fallen on hard times, losing both his wealth and his eyesight. In desperation, he prayed to God for relief, then decided to send his son to collect some money that he had given to a

LEFT: *Tobias and the Archangel Raphael* (detail) by **Antonio Pollaiolo (*c.*1432–98). Most paintings of this subject show Tobias accompanied by his dog.**

"The second is he who presides over every suffering and every wound of the sons of man, the holy Raphael."

1 Enoch 40.9

relative many years before for safekeeping. Tobias, wary of travelling alone, set out to find a guide. The archangel Raphael, in answer to Tobit's prayer, manifested himself as a man to become a travelling companion for Tobias. Before leaving, Raphael reassured the old man that a cure for his blindness would be found.

On the journey, Raphael told Tobias that he would marry Sarah, the daughter of his father's cousin. This news unnerved Tobias, who knew that Sarah had already been married seven times. Sarah, meanwhile, had been praying for her own salvation and an end to her torment. On the first night of each of her marriages her husband had been killed before their union could be consummated – by the demon Asmodeus, who wanted Sarah for himself.

As Tobias and Raphael rested beside a river, Tobias was attacked by a large fish. Raphael told Tobias how to free himself, and he quickly caught the fish. Raphael instructed Tobias to remove the fish's liver, heart and gall bladder, and keep them. They then cooked the fish and ate some, taking the remainder with them.

Upon reaching Sarah's house, Raphael told Tobias to burn the fish's liver and heart with incense in the bridal chamber, as this would keep away the demon. When Tobias saw Sarah he gladly agreed to marry her, and they wed successfully, thanks to Raphael's instruction. To show his delight Sarah's father gave the couple a 14-day wedding ceremony and half his wealth.

On returning to Tobit and his wife, Raphael told Tobias to put the gall bladder of the fish on his father's eyes; as he did so, his father's cataracts fell away and his sight was fully restored.

In appreciation of this miracle, Tobit offered Raphael half of the dowry. Raphael refused, saying that he was one of the seven great angels who hear and relay the prayers of the righteous to God. His parting instruction was that Tobit should write his story.

CHANNELLING HEALING ENERGY

It is said that we are all capable of healing – ourselves as well as others. If you wish to invite the archangel Raphael to use you as a channel for healing, all you really need at first is a genuine desire to be of true service.

There are many ways in which you can act as a channel for healing in the world. You might choose to join with others of like mind to send out prayers for the whole of humanity at a certain time of day. Perhaps you wish Raphael to be present as you send absent healing to others. When you are with someone who needs healing, you can place your hands on their head or shoulders, or wherever they are feeling pain. Simply open your heart to receive the healing energy of the angels and let it flow into the person you are touching.

You can also ask Raphael to heal your own pain, especially the emotional pain of broken relationships. Sit quietly and imagine a healing green light around you; absorb it through your whole body, especially into any areas of pain – whether in your body, or in your thoughts and emotions. Visualize angels passing over you and drawing the pain out of you with their hands.

The following exercise is a method for healing other people (though it can easily be adapted to be directed at healing yourself). The other people can be physically present with you, but this is not essential because the exercise is about channelling waves of healing energy and does not involve physical contact. As one "holds" the healing energy it is not uncommon to receive messages for the recipient. You may wish to share these at some point afterwards as they could be of great significance. Relate any messages as accurately as possible, without personal comment or advice – you are just the channel.

There is no set duration for this exercise, and it should last no more than 20 minutes. You will learn to sense when the session is over.

1 Sit comfortably in your meditational space and breathe slowly and deeply to release any tension held in your body, particularly in your neck, shoulders and hands.

2 Empty your mind of your own pre-occupations and focus on the needs of the person you wish to heal. Visualize the person in your mind if it helps.

3 Send a prayer in your own words to the Divine Source of all love and the master of healing. Ask that you may receive the grace to be used as a channel of healing energy, and that this energy may flow through you with love to the person who is sick or in pain.

4 Invite Raphael to draw near you – imagine that you can feel his presence. Visualize the colour green all around you as a beautiful healing light, balancing and harmonizing thoughts, words, and actions between you, the recipient, and Raphael.

5 Remain relaxed but focused. Open your heart so that it can give love unconditionally to the recipient. Visualize bright green light channelled through the crown of your head, flowing down through your heart and your hands and out to the one who needs healing, wherever they may be.

6 Observe silently any pictures, feelings or sensations that come into your mind. You may sense in your own body where the other person's pain is held. Remain silent and simply receive the healing energy channelling through you, allowing it to flow freely. Finish when you feel ready.

7 Thank Raphael and the angels of healing at the end of the session for their assistance.

URIEL

The archangel of salvation and ministration, Uriel embodies angelic energy relating to purity of the heart and true spiritual peace.

According to the Book of Enoch, Uriel was recognized, alongside Michael, Gabriel and Raphael, as one of the four angels of the Divine Presence, standing before God. And while he may be the least well known of the quartet, he remains nonetheless an angel of tremendous strength and influence.

Sometimes called Phanuel, the archangel Uriel is identified in other Jewish scriptures as the "fire of God". He is found in the Jewish, Kabbalist, Christian and Islamic traditions — although in 745CE his status as an archangel was revoked by the Christian Church because the clergy considered that the laity were showing too much devotion to angels, rather than the Holy Trinity.

RIGHT: *The Peace Angel* **(2003), as painted by contemporary artist Sue Jamieson.**

ARCHANGEL URIEL

ARCHANGEL OF PEACE, SALVATION AND MINISTRATION

DAY OF THE WEEK: Friday

ASSOCIATED COLOURS: gold, ruby red, purple

- Uriel's name means "fire of God", "flame of God", "light of God" or "sun of god".

- One of the four angels of the Divine Presence, the archangel is also ranked as a seraph and a cherub.

- Practically speaking, Uriel helps with peace, devotional worship, service, brotherhood, ministration and detachment.

- Uriel's assistance will help you to overcome emotional turbulence, egocentricity, conflict, harmfulness and desire.

Much of what we know of Uriel originates from rabbinical literature and non-canonical sources. He is not actually named in the Bible, although various acts which occur in the Old Testament are attributed to him.

In the Old Testament and Hebrew tradition Uriel is said to be the angel (in his role as a cherub) who stands at the gate to the Garden of Eden, wielding a sword of flame. Yet Uriel is also the angel who, as a result of his faithfulness and steadfast loyalty, presides over the entrance to hell (Tartarus, or Hades). In art he has frequently been depicted carrying a fiery sword in one hand, and the keys to hell in the other.

Uriel is believed to be the archangel who gave humankind the Kabbalah and disclosed the heavenly mysteries of the arcana (secret knowledge, often sought by alchemists in the Middle Ages) to Ezra. Thus artists have also depicted him carrying a book or papyrus scroll. Kabbalistic writings assign Uriel to the middle pillar of the Tree of Life, and specifically to the sephirah Malkuth, the Kingdom.

Uriel was the angel whom God sent to warn Noah of the impending Flood (but it was

LEFT: *An Angel holding an Olive Branch*, by Hans Memling (*c.*1433–94). The olive branch is a symbol of peace, harking back to the branch that was brought to Noah by the dove after the Flood.

Raphael who showed Noah how to build the ark), and to lead Abraham out of the city of Ur. It was Uriel who wrestled with Jacob in the Book of Genesis. In Jewish lore, he is considered one of the angels present at Adam's repentance and to have ministered at his burial.

In the second book of the Sibylline Oracles, which are a rather confusing blend of early Christian, Jewish and pagan prohecies, Uriel is said to be one of the "immortal angels of the undying God" who, on the Day of Judgment, will "break the monstrous bars framed of unyielding and unbroken adamant of the brazen gates of Hades, and cast them down straightway, and bring forth to judgment all the sorrowful forms."

There are also traces of Uriel's presence in apocalyptic literature. For example, in 2 Esdras (4.1–4), a series of apocalyptic visions of the end of time are presented through a dialogue between the prophet Ezra and the archangel Uriel. These visions are very similar to those found in the Book of Revelation in the New Testament and to others in a second-century Christian text, *Shepherd of Hermes*. The latter is not viewed as canonical by the Church, however, and its author is unknown:

"Then the angel that had been sent to me, whose name was Uriel, answered and said to me, 'Your understanding has utterly failed regarding this world, and do you think you can comprehend the way of the Most High?' Then I said, 'Yes, my lord.' And he replied to me, 'I have been sent to show you three ways, and to put before you three problems. If you can solve one of them for me, then I will show you the way you desire to see, and will teach you why the heart is evil.'"

As the archangel of peace, salvation and ministration Uriel ultimately leads us to Divine love and service to God. In Theosophy it is said that Uriel is connected to the sixth ray of devotion and idealism (see pages 70–1). You can work with Uriel to develop compassion, selflessness and inner peace. Uriel can also help you deal with conflict and anger. Traditionally regarded as the angel of the planet earth, Uriel is also the angel to invoke for care of animals and nature.

ENGAGING WITH THE ANGELS OF PEACE

The following meditation is designed to bring tranquillity of mind, and soothe friction within families. The archangel Uriel will work with us and through us if we allow ourselves to be used as channels for God's peace.

The frenetic pace of modern life can mean that we rarely experience true peace. Emotional distress caused by conflict in relationships also disturbs our equilibrium. But Divine forces of peace and forgiveness are always available to us.

This meditation is designed to help you consciously to release any disturbing feelings or resentments you hold, toward either yourself or others. They are unwanted in the role of peacemaker and will be a hindrance if you want to be a channel for Divine peace. Once these antagonistic feelings are dissolved, you are ready to actively become a channel of peace – for example, within your family, or between colleagues at work.

The beautiful prayer of St Francis of Assisi can be used regardless of your faith, Christian or otherwise. Try reading it whenever you are feeling unsettled.

Lord,
Make me an instrument of Thy peace,
Where there is hate may I bring love;
Where there is injury, pardon;
Where there is doubt, faith;
Where there is despair, hope;
Where there is darkness, light; and
Where there is sadness, joy.
Oh Divine Master,
Grant that I may not so much seek to be consoled, as to console;
To be understood as to understand;
To be loved as to love.
For it is in giving that we receive,
It is in pardoning that we are pardoned, and
It is in forgetting self that we are born to eternal life.

1 Settle into your own quiet space, and allow yourself simply to "be". Cross your hands in front of your heart for a moment, then release your hands and rest them on your lap, palms facing upward.

2 Concentrate on your breathing. Inhale deeply and, as you exhale, release the tension from your neck and shoulders, and the muscles throughout your body. Visualize your concerns being blown away and dissolved in a bright, loving light.

3 Repeat this slow, rhythmic breathing until you feel relaxed and calm. Now say to yourself, "Peace, be still. Peace, be still." Repeat as many times as it takes until you really *feel* the word "peace" resonating throughout your body and mind.

4 Concentrate on any areas of your body that remain uncomfortable, or any areas of conflict in your life that come to mind. These are the issues with which you humbly seek Uriel's assistance.

5 When you are ready, call the archangel Uriel by name, either in your head, or out loud if you feel comfortable with this. Now say the following three times:

> Uriel, and the angels of peace
> I am ready to accept the gift of peace
>   in my heart,
> Peace in my soul, peace in my spirit
>   and peace in my mind.
> Make me an instrument of God's peace!

6 Sit still for a few moments with the resulting feeling of peace, calm and serenity. Carry these feelings with you, and recall them at any time that you feel agitated.

CHAMUEL

Above all, Chamuel is the archangel of pure, unconditional love. In the angelic realm he oversees both divine love and divine justice.

One of the seven great archangels, the archangel Chamuel is chief of the Order of Powers in the angelic hierarchy; in the Kabbalist tradition he is one of the sefirot of the Tree of Life. Like Gabriel, Chamuel is considered to be one of the angels who was present at the Garden of Gethsemane when Jesus went there to meditate on his plight prior to his arrest and subsequent crucifixion. He is also said to have been one of the ministering angels who attended Jesus at the Resurrection.

Chamuel teaches us to expand our capacity to love, and the value of working with the best possible intentions, for the benefit of all mankind, not just ourselves.

RIGHT: *The Resurrection: the Angels rolling away the Stone from the Sepulchre*, **by William Blake. One of these angels is believed to have been Chamuel.**

ARCHANGEL CHAMUEL

ARCHANGEL OF LOVE

DAY OF THE WEEK: Tuesday

ASSOCIATED COLOUR: pink

• Chamuel's name means "He who sees God".

• The archangel Chamuel has large green wings, and is usually depicted in armour and wearing a red tunic.

• Practically speaking, Chamuel holds and represents the qualities of the Christ, including love, tolerance and gratitude, and can help us to overcome low self-esteem or a damaged heart.

• Chamuel helps us to find love, compassion, creativity and beauty in the people around us and in our surrounding environment.

VISUALIZING ANGELIC LOVE

Chamuel can help us nurture real love, both toward ourselves and, with this firm basis, toward others.

It is no coincidence that pink is the colour of love and the colour linked with Chamuel. All shades of pink represent love, both human and divine. Real love is strong and supportive; above all, it is grounded in self-love; it is loving a person without needing to control them, allowing them to be free; it is nurturing without smothering; it is being true to your soul.

Chamuel teaches us to show compassion and tolerance, toward ourselves as well as others. He can help to dissolve feelings of low self-esteem, and help us to accept and love ourselves fully. We can then move on to projecting this love

LEFT: **The Angel of Love (detail) from the *Roman de la Rose* (c.1487–95).**

toward others. Chamuel can help you to find true love in your relationships, which will be attracted into your life once you begin to practise tolerance and unconditional love toward yourself and those around you in your everyday actions.

Whenever your self-esteem is low, or you are tempted to be too harsh on yourself or on others, you will find the following meditation a useful foil to these negative thoughts. Make sure that you practise it with honest and loving intent, and with as open a heart as possible.

This may take some practice if you are holding negative energy that manifests itself as pain in a certain area of your body, or if you are unhappy with some aspect of your physical appearance. Rose quartz crystal enhances the loving energy of Chamuel. You can also light a candle if you wish.

1 Sit comfortably in a quiet space. Slowly move your concentration through your body, relaxing each set of muscles with each breath.

2 Ask the archangel Chamuel and the angels of love to come closer to you.

3 Imagine that you are surrounded by a beautiful swirling mist of pink light. Invite the light to enter your body. Visualize it filling your lungs and chest, then expanding through your entire body.

4 Concentrate on those areas the light does not seem to fill easily, and ask Chamuel to fill them with his loving light. Continue until every cell of your body is so full of the light that it starts radiating out from your skin.

5 Ask Chamuel to help you to dissolve any feelings of low self esteem, self-condemnation, or resentment toward others. Ask him to help you to create feelings of compassion, forgiveness, tolerance and gratitude toward yourself and everyone you meet.

6 Ask Chamuel to help you to attract loving and mutually beneficial relationships of friendship and love into your life.

7 Now imagine your heart as a beautiful pink rose. Infuse your heart with pink light and pure loving energy. If the rose you vizualize is a closed bud, allow Chamuel to encourage the bloom to unfurl and open its petals wide. Imagine that you can smell its fragrance; sense the perfect softness of each petal.

8 This purifying light of love is in your heart always. Carry it with you and draw upon it for the rest of the day.

JOPHIEL

Knowledge and wisdom — tempered with the benefits of creativity, insight and spiritual enlightenment — are the sources of Jophiel's energy.

A member of the cherubim, Jophiel is said to be the angel who drove Adam and Eve out of the Garden of Eden after they transgressed God's rules by eating the forbidden fruit. This would make him the first angel mentioned in the Bible (although not by name). According to Jewish belief, Jophiel is also seen as a companion to the archangel Metatron (see page 154).

As the angel of illumination, you can draw upon the energies of Jophiel to enlighten and inspire you. Jophiel's energy is particularly beneficial for teachers and students, and to anyone working in a creative field.

RIGHT: The Story of Adam and Eve (detail), from the book *Concerning the Fate of Illustrious Men and Women*, by the Italian storyteller Giovanni Boccaccio (1313–75).

ARCHANGEL JOPHIEL

ARCHANGEL OF ILLUMINATION

DAY OF THE WEEK: Monday

ASSOCIATED COLOUR: sunshine yellow

• Jophiel's name means "Beauty of God".

• Sometimes called Iofiel, Zophiel or Jofiel, Jophiel is the angel of art and beauty, and patron of artists.

• In Theosophy, the archangel Jophiel is believed to work with the ascended master Chohan Lanto on the second ray of Love-Wisdom (see pages 70–1).

• Practically speaking, working with the archangel Jophiel can bring wisdom, illumination, perception, clarity, inspiration, knowledge, intelligence and insight. Jophiel can help you to overcome ignorance, pride, mental confusion, and narrow-mindedness.

SEEKING CLARITY AND INSIGHT

Clearing the mind of clutter, and opening up to new sources of knowledge can benefit every one of us. The archangel Jophiel can help you to learn what you need in order to develop clear thinking, deeper understanding and foresight.

When seeking to develop truthfulness, understanding and creative intuition, Jophiel is the archangel to work with. Invoking Jophiel's wisdom and illumination can help you to find and remain on the correct and true path.

You could be studying for exams, or need guidance and clarity on how to stand up for a cause which you believe in. You may need to write an important letter and be unsure of how to get your point across, or perhaps you wish to pass on important principles or beliefs to others truthfully and tactfully.

The following exercise is designed to be used when you are feeling confused or lacking in knowledge. It can dissipate any negativity that is clouding your thinking and help you to assimilate information.

In step 6 of this exercise, if there is a particular issue that you would like guidance with, visualizing the letter, book, examination or situation in a physical form, and imagining your hands holding this out to Jophiel, will concentrate the focus of your request. If your issue is an idea or principle, you can visualize it in terms of key words or concepts appearing to you as if on flash cards.

In step 8 of the exercise you will visualize a yellow light concentrating into a narrow thread. Do not visualize this thread disappearing completely. Allow it to remain in your mind's eye as a constant connection between you and the Divine Source of insight. You can then carry the benefits of this exercise with you as you continue your daily activities.

1 Light a candle and sit comfortably, with your back straight. Breathe deeply and relax, releasing any tension with every exhalation.

2 Imagine a beautiful radiant yellow light surrounding you. Breathe the light in and see it filling your body with every breath. Draw the yellow light through your body and down into your arms, hands, legs and feet as you breathe, so that it completely fills your being.

3 Visualize the light seeping from your pores and out through the crown of your head, cascading down and around you like a brilliant swirling yellow mist.

4 Now imagine a beam of this radiant light shining upwards from the crown of your head, through the roof and into the sky, travelling like a laser beam through the clouds, the stars and finally connecting with the Source of all light and understanding.

5 Lovingly ask permission of the Source to commune with the archangel Jophiel and the angels of illumination, so that you may be blessed with understanding, creativity, and clarity of thought and communication.

6 If you are seeking guidance about a specific issue, visualize it in physical form and hold it out to Jophiel in your hands.

7 Remain sitting in the yellow light for as long as you wish. When you are ready, thank Jophiel with all your heart.

8 Visualize the yellow light gradually fading and the beam between the crown of your head and the Source narrowing until it appears as a thread of light, keeping you connected. Breathe deeply and bring your attention back to your body, your hands and feet, and your face. Open your eyes and be conscious again of your surroundings.

ZADKIEL

The violet flame of Zadkiel represents the transformative power of joy.
It can help you to release negativity and engender more positive feelings.

In Rabbinical writing, Zadkiel is the archangel of benevolence, mercy and memory. He is also represented in the Zohar, the main scriptural text of the Kabbalah, where he is one of the two chieftains (the other being Jophiel) who assist the archangel Michael, bearing his standard and following him directly into battle.

Zadkiel works with the violet flame, which can transform negative into positive energy – perhaps you are feeling pessimistic about a relationship, or disappointed with something at work. Even if circumstances prevent you following this exercise in full – such as the fact that you are in a noisy shopping centre – you can still seek Zadkiel's help. Stop for a moment, and visualize the violet flame surrounding you. Take deep breaths, releasing any negative thoughts or frustrations into the purifying flame, then thank Zadkiel for his assistance.

ARCHANGEL ZADKIEL

ARCHANGEL OF JOY

DAY OF THE WEEK: Saturday

ASSOCIATED COLOUR: violet

• Zadkiel's name means "righteousness of God".

• One of the seven angels in the presence of God, Zadkiel is ruler of the planet Jupiter.

• Some sources claim it was Zadkiel who prevented Abraham from killing his son Isaac as a sacrifice to God. As a result, he is often depicted holding a dagger.

• Practically speaking, Zadkiel helps with refinement, tolerance, transmutation (the change from negative to positive energy), forgiveness and diplomacy. He helps to overcome servitude or bondage, intolerance, dogmatism and hardness of heart.

VISUALIZING THE VIOLET FLAME

1 Sit comfortably on a chair, with your spine as straight as possible and your feet firmly on the floor. Breathe deeply and slowly.

2 Visualize stepping into a circle of violet flame, and see the flames rise all around you.

3 Feel the violet flame on the soles of your feet. Visualize the heat rising through your legs, filling your whole body. Draw the violet flame through you as you breathe in. Start to release your feelings of negativity and see them dissolve in the warm light of the flames. The flames purify you as they rise through your chest and you slowly breathe them out.

4 Next, allow the flame to purify your heart. Release a painful memory, or feelings of self-doubt. Imagine the flame melting away old scars you may be holding in your heart.

5 Next, visualize the flame rising to your neck, cleansing your throat of speaking unkind or negative words. Ask that all you communicate from now on be truthful and positive.

6 Now imagine the violet flame flowing up into your head. Allow the flame to purify your thought processes, enabling you to discern all that is good and true.

7 Finally, immerse yourself in the joy of the angels. Allow the violet flame to withdraw from your body through the soles of your feet.

8 Sit quietly, acknowledging your positive state of heart and mind. Thank Zadkiel, and ask for his continued assistance in dissolving any further negative feelings as they arise through the day.

METATRON

Metatron differs in several ways from the other archangels. He is considered the most powerful of them all, and the closest to God.

Most of what we believe today about the archangel Metatron springs from Jewish mysticism. There seems to be no real agreement over why the name "Metatron" differs so greatly from the names of the other archangels, lacking as it does the usual suffix *-el* (of God). One interpretation is that the name derives from the Latin *metator*, meaning a "guide" or "measure".

But Metatron is also known in some strands of Jewish mysticism as "lesser YHWH". The word "YHWH" is Hebrew and symbolizes the sacred and unutterable name of God. This ties in with the belief that Metatron occupies the throne next to the Divine throne and resides with God in the seventh heaven. He has also been called the King of Angels, Prince of the Divine Face, and Angel of the Covenant. In fact Metatron is thought of as being so mighty that he possesses 72 names altogether.

In many non-canonical writings, Metatron is considered to be the highest and most powerful in the celestial hierarchy. He is one of the select few who is allowed to look directly upon God's face, something which is denied even to some of the other archangels. But how else does Metatron stand apart from the other archangels?

One important difference is the fact that he was once human, an attribute shared by only one other angel, Sandalphon, who was once the prophet Elijah. According to Genesis (5.24), Enoch "walked with God; then he was no more, because God took him." From this brief verse arose an elaborate legend: that of the patriarch Enoch, a humble, pious mortal who, according to tradition, so pleased God in his abilities as a scribe, and with his honesty and goodness, that he was transported to heaven and made into an archangel, Metatron. Upon arrival Enoch was equipped with 36 pairs of wings and innumerable eyes.

The traditional story of Enoch as Metatron is important in Merkabah mysticism, in which 3 Enoch is a key text. According to Rabbinical literature Enoch was raised to the rank of first of the angels and Mynph, which literally means "Prince of the Divine Face", or "Divine Presence". The Merkabah emphasizes his role as the knower of secrets, able both to receive and transmit mysteries between humanity and the angels, and vice versa. The Talmud places Metatron as the direct link between God and humankind. Further, in 3 Enoch 38 Metatron tells Rabbi Ishmael that it was he who revealed the Ten Commandments to Moses. In Kabbalist lore it is Metatron who leads the children of Israel through the wilderness.

In the same Rabbinical literature we find that Enoch was given some preparation for his role as Metatron, first from the angel Vereveil,

RIGHT: *The Recording Angel* (**Metatron**) one of **William Blake's illustrations for the** *Divine Comedy* **by Dante (1265–1321).**

who instructs him in all the ways of the Lord. Enoch is then instructed on the earth, the sea, the elements and the courses; Hebrew and all the other languages; and everything that is appropriate to learn. Secondly, we are told that God continued to instruct Enoch in secrets that he had not explained even to the angels. Following this instruction Enoch is given the role of "scribing everything that happens on earth and in the heavens, and being a witness of the judgment, of the great age" (2 Enoch 36:3).

Interestingly, in some later writings Enoch is described as having the title of Metatron Na'ar, the latter word meaning "youth". The possible explanation for this is that Metatron is indeed young when compared to the other archangels, who have been in existence since the beginning of Creation.

Metatron is the recorder of all events that occur in the universe, in both the heavenly and earthly realms, and is overseer of the angel keepers of the Akashic records. As overlighting angel of the first Sefirah of the Kabbalah, Metatron represents the Keter, or Crown. (see page 101).

Sandalphon

The spiritual twin brother of Metatron, Sandalphon is the only other angel to have once been human – he was the Prophet Elijah. After being transported to heaven in a chariot, Elijah is said to have remained there as an archangel, in order to be of further service to God.

Sandalphon is one of the tallest of the angels according to Jewish lore. He is so tall that when Moses was taken to receive the Torah in the third heaven he was struck with fear at his size. Sandalphon is said to be instrumental in differentiating the sex of the unborn, and stands at the crossroads of Paradise helping the righteous to find heaven after death. Sandalphon assists Michael in the ceaseless battle against Samma'el, Satan's chief angel of darkness.

Currently Sandalphon is often represented as a strong, loving feminine energy, primarily acting as a guide through spiritual crises.

RIGHT: *Abraham and the Three Angels*, a Macedonian icon *c.*1700. The angels foretold the birth of Isaac, and some sources claim it was Metatron who later prevented Abraham from sacrificing his son.

BIBLIOGRAPHY

Aquinas, St Thomas, *Summa Theologiae* Volume 9 (ia. 50–64): Angels, (ed. and trans. Kenelm Foster) London: Blackfriars/Eyren Spottiswoode; New York: McGraw Hill (1968)

Bernstein, Henrietta, *Cabalah Primer*, California: De Vorss & Co (1984)

Carey, Jacqueline, *Angels: Celestial Spirits in Legend and Art*, New York: Metro Books (1997)

Church, Anthea, *Angels*, London: Brahma Kumaris (1997)

Cohn, Norman, *Cosmos, Chaos & the World to Come*, London: Yale University Press (1995)

Connelly, Douglas, *Angels Around Us: What the Bible Really Says*, Illinois: Intervarsity Press (1994)

Cortens, Theolyn, *Living with Angels*, London: Piatkus Books (2003)

—, *The Angel's Script*, Oxford: Caer Sidi Publications (1997)

Dadi Janki, *Wings of Soul*, London: Brahma Kumaris (1998)

Daniel, Alma, Timothy Wyllie, and Andrew Ramer, *Ask your Angels*, Canada: Ballantine Books (1992); London: Piatkus Books (1995)

Davidson, Gustav, *A Dictionary of Angels*, New York: Simon & Schuster (1967)

Fox, Leonard, and Donald L. Rose, eds., *Conversations with Angels: What Swedenborg Heard in Heaven*, (David Gladish and Jonothan Rose trans.), London: Chrysalis Books (1996)

Godwin, Malcolm, *Angels: an Endangered Species*, New York: Simon & Schuster (1990)

Graham, Billy, *Angels: God's Secret Agents*, London: Hodder & Stoughton (1986)

Heathcote-James, Emma, *Seeing Angels*, London: John Blake Publishing (2001)

Hodson, Geoffrey, *The Kingdom of Gods*, London: Theosophical Publishing (1976)

—, *The Brotherhood of Angels and of Men*, London: Theosophical Publishing (1927)

Huyssen, Chet and Lucile, *Visions of Jesus*, New Jersey: Logos (1977)

Kessler, Michael and Christian Sheppard, eds., *Mystics, Presence and Aporia*, Chicago: University of Chicago Press (2003)

MacEwen, Anne, *Stepping Stones to a New Understanding*, Englang Publishing (1991)

McIntosh, J. ed., *Angels, a Joyous Celebration*, Philadelphia: Courage Books (1996)

Moolenburgh, H.C., *Meetings with Angels*, Essex: C. W. Daniel Co (1992)

—, *A Handbook of Angels*, Essex: C. W. Daniel Co (1993)

Pearson, Gena ed., *Cherubs, a Joyous Celebration*, Philadelphia: Courage Books (1998)

Porter, J.R., *The Lost Bible*, London: Duncan Baird Publishers (2001)

Price, Hope, *Angels*, London: Macmillan (1993)

Price, John Randolph, *The Angels Within Us*, London: Piatkus Books (1993)

Printz, Thomas, *The Mighty Elohim Speak*, California: Bridge to Freedom, (1957)

—, *The Seven Beloved Archangels Speak*, California: Ascended Master Teaching Foundation (1954)

Prophet, Elizabeth Clare, *How to Work with Angels*, Montana: Summit University Press (1998)

Roland, Paul, *Kabbalah*, London: Piatkus Books (1999)

Serres, Michel, *Angels: A Modern Myth*, France: Flammarion (1993)

Szekely, Edmond Bordeaux, *The Gospel of the Essenes*, Essex: C. W. Daniel Co (1974)

Wauters, Ambika, *The Angel Oracle: Working with the Angels for Guidance, Inspiration and Love*, London: Connections Book Publishing (1996)

—, *The Angelic Year*, London: Carroll & Brown (2000)

White, Ruth, *Working with Guides and Angels*, London: Piatkus Books (1996)

INDEX

ACKNOWLEDGMENTS

The publisher would like to thank the following people, museums, and photographic libraries for permission to reproduce their material. Every care has been taken to trace copyright holders. However, if we have omitted anyone we apologize and will, if informed, make corrections to any future edition.

All these images have been supplied by The Bridgeman Art Library, London
a = above, b = below
Agnew & Sons, London 53; All Saints Church, Selsley, Gloucestershire 55; American Illustrators Gallery, New York 68; Ashmolean Museum, University of Oxford 83; Bibliothèque Nationale, Paris 74, 75a+b, 122; Birmingham Museum and Art Gallery 16-17, 154, 155; Bradford Art Galleries and Museums 8; British Library, London 34, 35, 146; Christie's Images, London 46-47, 116a+b; Christopher Wood Gallery, London 67; Dulwich Picture Gallery, London 104, 105; Fitzwilliam Museum, University of Cambridge 58, 59, 106, 107; Galleria Nazionale dell'Umbria, Perugia 128; Uffizi, Florence 14b, 23, 112, 113; Galleria Sabauda, Turin 134; Kunsthalle, Hamburg 64, 65; Hotel Dieu, Beaune 38, 39; Institute of Oriental

Studies, St Petersburg 40, 41; Koninklijk Museum voor Schone Kunsten, Antwerp 126, 127; Lambeth Palace Library, London 110-111; Louvre, Paris 2, 3a, 26, 27, 28, 29, 56, 57, 140; Musée Condé, Chantilly 102, 103, 148, 149; Musée des Beaux-Arts Thomas Henry, Cherbourg 88; Musée des Beaux-Arts, Blois 94, 95; Musée des Beaux-Arts, Lyons 3b, 20, 21, 22, 37, 90, 130; Museo Arcivescovile, Ravenna 6, 7; Museo Civico, Padua 80, 86, 87,; Museo di San Marco dell'Angelico, Florence 84; Museo Diocesano de Lérida, Catalonia 14a, 15; Museo Figline, Valdagno 93; National Gallery, London 78, 79; Oriental Museum, Durham University 30a, 31; Palazzo Medici-Riccardi, Florence 48, 49, 114, 115; Prado, Madrid 44, 45, 117-118; Private Collections 1, 30b, 36, 70, 73, 77, 97, 109, 120, 121, 138, 139; Richardson and Kailas Icons, London 157; Santuario Santa Casa, Loreto 50, 51; Santuario Santa Maria delle Grazie, Saronno 18-19; Santa Maria della Vittoria, Rome 60, 61; Scrovegni (Arena) Chapel, Padua 24, 25; Seattle Art Museum 32a+b, 33; Sudley House, Liverpool 12, 13; The Barnes Foundation, Merion, Pennsylvania 132, 133; Collégiale Notre-Dame, Huy 99; Victoria & Albert Museum, London 5, 10, 42, 63, 144, 145

Every care has been taken to trace copyright holders to secure permission to quote from their sources. We apologize if any have been omitted and will gladly correct any future editions if so informed.

The scripture quotations contained herein are from the New Revised Standard Version Bible, © 1989 by the division of Christian Education of the National Council of the Churches of Christ in the USA. All rights reserved.

Other non-canonical extracts are taken from the standard scholarly collections of the *Pseudepigrapha* by J. H. Charlesworth ed. (London: Darton, Longman and Todd, 1983) and of the *New Testament Apocrypha* by W. Schneelmelcher ed. 2 vols., (Cambridge: James Clarke and Co 1991–2).

The extract on page 96 is from *The Complete Dead Sea Scrolls* in English, ed and trans by Geza Vermes, Penguin 1998.

The Essene Invocations on page 98 are from Anne MacEwen, *Stepping Stones to a New Understanding* (see Bibliography).